YO-BSY-572

SOME
ACQUIRED
TASTES

JURGEN GOTHE

SOME
ACQUIRED
TASTES
A RECIPE ALBUM

DOUGLAS & McINTYRE
VANCOUVER/TORONTO

Copyright © 1995 by Jurgen Gothe
Photographs © by Kate Williams

95 96 97 98 99 5 4 3 2 1

All rights reserved. No part of this book may be reproduced, stored in a retrieval system
or transmitted in any form or by any means without the prior permission of the publisher
or, in the case of photocopying or other reprographic copying, a licence from CANOPY
(Canadian Repography Collective, Toronto, Ontario).

Douglas & McIntyre
1615 Venables Street
Vancouver, British Columbia
V5L 2H1

Canadian Cataloguing in Publication Data

Gothe, Jurgen, 1944-
Some acquired tastes

ISBN 1-55054-429-2

1. Cookery. I. Title.
TX714.G67 1995   641.5   C95-910539-5

Editing by Elizabeth Wilson
Cover and text design by DesignGeist
Cover and text illustration by Michael J. Downs
Printed and bound in Canada by Best Book Manufacturers

The publisher gratefully acknowledges the assistance of the
Canada Council and of the British Columbia Ministry of
Tourism, Small Business and Culture for its publishing programs.

WITH LOVE TO ALL THOSE
WHO'VE EATEN AT—
AND UNDER—MY TABLE.

CONTENTS

Acknowledgements

Thank you, thank you, thank you all ...

... in the first place, the trio that brings me love and laughter and lots of other goodies: Kate, Colette and Herbie the cat

... then Mrs. B. for input and output; throughput—some days, I shouldn't wonder, even shotput—for propelling this into being

... to say nothing of Scott McIntyre in observance of the fact we've been at this for longer than 66 per cent of all marriages, 73 per cent of all businesses and 96 per cent of all restaurants

... and of course the boys and girls in the band, who ride the airwaves with me most afternoons, the DiscDrive unit: Janet Lea and David Fedoruk, Michael Juk and Grant Rowledge (and all the others who got on and off along the way); Ede Wouk, naturally, with special thanks for his title work—I'm just sorry we couldn't come up with a good hyphenate

... not forgetting Mr. Bill and Mr. Bird and ABC and the Willsons; the other regular and faithful, uncomplaining tasters, even if I did have to persuade you with high-end chardonnay now and then

... Elizabeth Wilson for braving these troubled typographic waters yet again, with grace and style and cheer

... Saeko Usukawa and Terri Wershler and all of the D&M mobilizers and achievers and getter-doners; Gabi Proctor and Sigrid Albert, the meisterdesigngeisters; Marg Meikle, the index lady, whose position as paramount indexer of culinary volumes by CBC personalities seem unassailable

... Kate Williams (there she is again) for never saying "Smile!"

... naturally, all the chefs herein and elsewhere, professional and amateur, who agreed to let me mess with their recipes: all the wine people and food folks and restaurant regulars; all the listeners, viewers and readers who listened, watched and read and helped supply sources, selection, ideas, encouragement, comments.

In a mega-nutshell, then: Othmar Steinhart, Bernard Plé and Heinrich Fischer; Daniel Mirassou and all the Mirassou Vineyards bunch; Wolfgang von Wieser, Kerry Sear and Ruy Paes-Braga; Robert Le Crom; Otto Bjornson and Anja Vogels; Renee Carisio and Janet Trefethen; Frank Valoczy; Alan Groom and Eleni Skalbania; Sharon and Ken Wildwind; Kam Shing Lam and Simon Lee

. . . Ken Bogas, Dan Atkinson, Brent Wolrich and Brendan Mann, Anne Milne, Claude St. Onge and Shirley and Leon Sobon, Bernard Casavant, Andrew and Deborah Cutter and the cats, Mildred Howie, Dagobert Niemann, Gianni Picchi, Patricia Maynard Sloan (and the WPFD), Armando Diaz

. . . Karen Barnaby, Paul MacEwen, Elizabeth Fox and Greg Hays, Gildo Casadei and all the Casadeis, Janice Lotzkar, Sue Adams, Doug Porter and Mario Enero, Manuel Ferreira, Peter Burge and Hubert Schmid

. . . Don McDougall, Amyn Sunderji, Tina Perenseff and John Bishop, Emily Goetz, Patrice Suhner, Monique Barbeau (and Lou Richmond for all his facilitating), Hart Melvin, Rodney Butters, Pierre Delacôte, Corinne Poole, Michael Lyons and Jill Pike, Ernst Dörfler, Irene Hain, Jayne Wagner, Vicki Gabereau

. . . William Mark (*The Chinese Gourmet,* Raincoast Distributors, 1994) and Hugh Quetton (*I'll Drink to That,* Toronto, H.Q. Services, 1992) for permission to quote or paraphrase from their books

. . . and last, but maybe most important, you for stopping by here today. Let's get something to eat, shall we?

Introduction

Now it begins—The Big Eat.

Welcome. I hope you'll add as much avoirdupois as I did, finding all these recipes; it's a process not without its own elements of fun and entertainment.

Some of the 101 are mine—the ones without a name at the top under the title—others are others'. Ultimately I am taking responsibility for the lot though, because at one time or another, in some form or another, they've all gone through me, you should pardon the term.

This inevitability—The Cookbook— came about as a result of my long-time, long-suffering assistant, Mrs. Brown, sitting in her office one morning, training for the bridge tournament or whatever it is she does with that computer, swirling a julep in her monogrammed mug, the mail not in yet, wondering how many recipes J.G. had run in his columns over the years. And she inveigled the computer into joining her in that greatest of all German pastimes, making a list, and I looked at it and put it away somewhere in the sort of place I put things away—one of the Big Boxes.

Months passed. Maybe a year. One day I started to notice the absence of a book with my name on it out there. The last publisher I'd been with had just offered to destroy the remaining copies of my previous paperback at no direct cost to me. After telling me last year, when I could have sold some, there weren't any left—I guess they've got The Big Boxes in inaccessible places too. It's an odd business.

No, there wasn't a volume of words to be accessed, unless you went to that wonderful new Vancouver library where their computer listed no less than a dozen copies of Good Gothe available for the asking, and two of them out.

Bless you, dear borrowers.

So maybe a cookbook? Everybody has these cookbooks, even Vicki Gabereau who professes not to cook, but I know better. So I leaped astride the new intrusion technology and put a fax into the corporate midst of Scott McIntyre's publishing company, saying let's do a quick one and put it into people's stockings for Christmas.

That was in the early part of 1994. He responded in his traditional-and-bless-him-for-it way: let's have lunch. A number of enjoyable lunches—at least one of them leading to a recipe herein—eventually led to a launch.

I have written a few million words over the last thirty-something years and most of them have had to do with food and drink in some way, and I still do love to cook—and often—and apart from some Texas chili afterburn or serious garlic overload, no one seems to have suffered at these hands. So here it is then. I'm actually prouder of it than I like to let on.

You may find that not all these recipes follow homemakers' form, to say nothing of Canada's Food Rules! I know the publishers have enlisted the services of various professionals who must surely have wondered a hundred times what they'd gotten themselves in for. I hope we got all the yellow sticky notes out, but if there are any left, follow those rather than my text.

Rule #1: if there's any confusion, go with your gut. Then, yes, you can write me in care of the publisher and I'll see what I can do about fixing it for the Portuguese edition. Or the movie. Keanu will take the role of the tuna casserole.

But at some time these recipes have all been prepared by me, in my kitchen. Many of them many times. If there remains anything I forgot, overlooked, left out, put in the wrong place, unintentionally quadrupled by an errant keystroke—you blame me, not the editor, not the homemaker, not the metrifier, not the list-of-ingredients-maker, not the indexer, not the publisher, not the designer, not the chefs who did their best and not the cat. Me.

If you do write, please, please don't ask me about the magnum of '58 Château de Former Self you have under the stairs by the stack of Geographics from the '60s, because I won't know. But I think you probably should have opened it on Bradley's birthday like you were planning.

Rule #23: don't try any of these for company without trying them on yourself and the immediate family, or the dog, first. Just in case. Once in a Vancouver Sun "Carte Blanche" column I offered Charles Saunders's fabulous

Sonoma buttermilk foie gras biscuits recipe to my readers. It came out with way too much buttermilk and not enough flour; the result was a lovely, expensive liver-slush/soup. Dozens of cats about town were ecstatic. Their keepers less so. These things happen.

Let me now, speaking of cats, dispel a nasty rumour going round: "I under-stand you don't really have cats," people come up to me and say after the symphony, at readings, in restaurants, remotes, retreats, road-races, raisers of funds—even Air Canada's #136, out first thing in the morning to Toronto.

Do, too!

I don't know how that got started but it isn't true; at least one place in this book you'll find the famous Herbie the Cat: megaManx, morning loudmouth, frantic foodie himself. Say hello, Herbie.

In my defense, before you say anything, I'll tell you this is a well-inten-tioned cookbook; the heart is in the right place. It may be a little harder to find it, with the butter and the cream, and if some things don't work for your diet, feel free to substitute lesser offenders. And don't forget to drink more red wine and eat more olives.

Another thing: I cook with spoons and cups, splodges and glops and shots and such; never mLs or gs or all those agents of science. Someone else kindly con-verted it all and I'm grateful and I'm sure it will work. You see, I had to learn all that business once, in school when I was a tyke. Then I had to unlearn it all over a single summer when I came here and get into the imperial material. That's enough; damned if I'll do it again. It's my kitchen and I'll fry if I want to.

There are 101 recipes identified, and quite a few hidden on or about the text. They've come from all over. People send me things. Others I ask for when I eat something really good. I don't actively collect them; I just stick 'em in my pocket and hope to be able to read them at some point. Still others I invent when the muse drops by for lunch.

I find it difficult to think about inventing recipes. You never know when it might happen; I never set out to do it. Usually, I find myself halfway down a bottle of pinot blanc and midway through making the meal when something flashes and suggests it might be worth keeping.

Now to backtrack: try and remember what's gone in the pot so far and how much of it. My recipes are more reliable from the halfway point on; the earlier bits are subject to considerable interpretation.

Rule #11: feel free to adapt and alter anything, anytime. You can credit me if you feel generous, otherwise put the book away and tell them you made it up yourself, especially if they like it. Show me the cook who doesn't. How many times have you been to dinner at someone's house and everything is tasty and wonderful and the cook says, "Yes, the sauce is on Page 105 of Craig's Big Apple cookbook, and the meat's done according to Jacques . . . " Well, not! People smile a little and say, "Oh, you like it? I've been perfecting it for quite a while now . . . "

We have all tried very hard, in the interests of fairness and credit where credit's due, to locate all original sources for the recipes that aren't mine. Proof, as they say, is on file. If one fell through the grill, let me apologize now.

So why are there twelve sections? One for each apostle, one for each month of the year, one for each sign of the zodiac—I don't know! It just fell together that way. **Soups** *to start things: I love soup as a meal and I think the old adage is true, about only the pure in heart being able to make great soups. If some of these don't work, check your purity level.*

Bread *and baking could have taken up the next hundred pages instead of ten or twelve. Bread and cheese would surely be the most difficult things for me to cut from my diet, so I don't intend to. More red wine here, waiter. If I win the lottery and get to take the rest of my life off, I'll enroll in a serious baking course at once. The conducting lessons can come after that.*

Pasta *is what I probably eat most of. When the Child of the House was younger she would basically eat only beige food. That covered most of the world's pasta, and while today she's much further along the spectrum, even into the infra-red, there remains a strong fondness for pasta. Me too. A couple of these were especially created by me for her.*

Fish *I love but don't eat often enough. I don't know why either, Captain Highliner. Chicken is versatile and easy and tasty and so are some of the other* **fowl**. *The unrepentant carnivore is indulged next, as I turn my copy of Absolute*

Torch and Twang to the wall for a moment. I'm glad other people have opinions, that's what makes the world happen and I will always respect theirs. I expect them to respect mine. You can skip this section if you don't do **meat** *and still won't go hungry.*

A whole section about **oysters***? You know, there aren't a lot of oyster recipe books out there. Coming to love them relatively late in life, well past thirty, I enjoy them with missionary zeal. The best I ever ate? Easy: a cassoulet of oysters, watercress and John Dory, with pepper and Champagne, at The Pierrot in the Mandarin in Hong Kong. Fresh from the water, only yards away, with Beamish Stout and a tot of the Jameson, warm brown bread and butter, at Finin's in Midleton, County Cork. As part of the world's best oyster stew, at The Tampa Bay Wharf in the Tampa airport, Florida. In a simple "swimming soup" with black pepper, watercress and swirls of egg, alongside a lot of Lanson Champagne, at L'Auberge du Grand Cerf, in Montchenot, on the Route d'Épernay. And at various locations in Stanley Park, Victoria, Whistler and points north, east, west and south.*

I think along with the aforementioned bread and cheese, **stews** *are my favorite food, as a package. They're fun to make—easy and flexible, creative, expandable to accommodate any number of eaters. They fill the house with nice smells and you can keep eating them for days. I always like to have two happening, in repertory. (I like to leapfrog leftovers: won't eat the same stew two days in a row, but skip a day and I'll happily eat that way for weeks. Just a quirk.)*

Then **veggies** *galore, because nothing's worse than a wonderful meal with a bundle of limp-steamed beans, dead-plain alongside. Vegetables should get as much attention as any aspect of a meal and I love any restaurant that does that for me. Then some* **drinks***, alcoholic or not, including a couple of cooling favorites from a summer past.*

Desserts, naturally, for I have a great sweet tooth and I feel the one area in which many Canadian restaurants still disappoint is dessert creativity. Cheesecake, sorry, just can't cut it.*

And finally, some **stuff***—things that chanced along and had to go somewhere: tourtière crust, tuna sandwiches, basil dressing, corncob jelly.*

Somebody—no names, please—wanted me to put music suggestions in. I pushed the parameters with wine suggestions (many of which aren't wine) and catch-all "accompaniments."

The well-run kitchen is filled with sounds that emerge according to heart not head. Forget the obvious things people are always trying to foist off—they don't work, they don't connect: the Bach Coffee Cantatas and the Gottschalk cakewalks, the Trout Quintet, the Champagne Galop, the symphony La Poule. Milhaud's Le Boeuf sur le toit, for heaven's sake. It's all head stuff and there's not much headroom in my musical kitchen. It's way too visceral, which is why the well-stocked kitchen requires generous amounts of jazz, rock 'n' roll, country, blues, bluegrass, classical big and small; Oscar Peterson as well as Glenn Gould to grunt along with. But not so much Beethoven as La Bottine souriante.

There, that's one.

Plus: Paul Schoenfield's Parables, the Kronos Quartet's Africa album, Purcell's Fairy Queen, Tuva throat singers, Lyle Lovett, Glenn Gould's Byrd and Gibbons, Corky Siegel's harmonica chamber-blues ensemble, Mendelssohn's Midsummernight's Dream, (you won't do much better than the OSM and Dutoit, either), and Doug Cox's dobro. Cecilia Bartoli's Mozart, Anderson & Brown, Phil Alvin's 21st century blues, Merle Haggard, Mickey Katz, Don Byron, Kathy Geisler's electric Vivaldi or Bach, Beausoleil, The Chieftains, and Anne Sofie von Otter singing Berlioz, or Weill.

Jeff Healey, Alan Hovhaness, Diana Krall, Pierre Boulez, Fontella Bass, The Chenille Sisters, Il Giardino Armonico's Four Seasons, Don Ross, The Hilliard Ensemble, and Mark O'Connor's fiddling. Mahler's 4th, Those Darn Accordions!, Kirk Eliot's Druids at the Disco, The The's Hank Williams covers, Oudi Hrant, Martha Argerich, Big Daddy, Terry Riley's Rainbow in Curved Air, Gene Di Novi, and Scarlatti sonatas on the harp.

Maxim Vengerov, Joseph Spence, Lena Willemark and Ale Möller, Stan Kenton's collection of national anthems of the world, The Nuclear Whales Saxophone Orchestra, Schoenberg's Gurrelieder, Dick Hyman, Philip Glass, Herb Ellis, the Count Basie Big Band. Kim Kashkashian, Kelly Joe Phelps, Harp Dog Brown, Tongan brass music, Nathan Milstein, Ry Cooder, Janáček's

Sinfonietta, Sabine Meyer, Mozart's Eine Kleine Nachtmusik done big (Cleveland Orchestra) or small (Hagen Quartet), and Finjan's Selkirk Avenue klezmer.

Die Schöne Müllerin, Hawaiian slack-key guitar, Evelyn Glennie, Dawn Upshaw, Mingus, Mannheim Steamroller, the original London cast of Return to the Forbidden Planet, Mose Allison, the L.A. Guitar Quartet, and Richard Stoltzman. Songs of the Auvergne, Cesaria Evora, Ken Hyder and the World's Smallest Pipe Band, John Prine, Jubilant Sykes's spirituals, the MJQ, Lieutenant Kijé Suite, Värttinä, The Cranberries and Milladoiro.

Thomas Hampson, The Ukulele Orchestra of Great Britain, Hermann Baumann, Peter Sellers, Maddy Prior, The Barra MacNeils, Al Kooper, Scheherazade, pibroch, and Praetorius dances. The Penguin Café Orchestra, Gorecki's Totus tuus, Kathryn Tickell, Pinky and the Brains' Bubba Bo Bob Brain song, Jonathan and Darlene Edwards, Jean-Jacques Kantorow and the Paganini Ensemble, Sam Pilafian and Frank Vignola's Travelin' Light, Bessie Griffin and The Gospel Pearls, David Thomas Roberts's new rags, the Dvořák Bagatelles for harmonium and strings.

And—The Wild Bunnies of Kitsilano, naturally, by Rick Scott and his friends.

There it is then, I think it's 101; they just came rolling out as the paper kept rolling in. Now match one to each dish. No prizes, but good noise and good eats. Which is what it's all about then, isn't it. Enjoy yourself.

Jurgen Gothe

West Vancouver, the summer of '95.

P.S.: As we go to press, that new Danish doctors' study is just out: three to five glasses of wine a day is about right, according to the researchers, and while red's best, white helps the old ticker too. Makes sense to me, we have corpuscles of both official colors.

So change all the wine suggestions in the book to read: three glasses of Château Pétrus and call me in the morning.

SOUPS

*I think the old adage is
true, about only the
pure in heart being able
to make great soups.*

2

Green Pea and Clam Bisque with Bubbly

Mirassou Vineyards, San Jose, California

I remember the day a new batch of recipes arrived from my winemaking friends at Mirassou—and I couldn't get past this first one for months! There were twenty more in the stack but this bisque with bubbly was so tasty and so easy I didn't see much reason to move on to Number 2. As long as you have some sparkling wine in the house you can whip it up in a few minutes. While it will serve four, they have to be decorous eaters; the quantities aren't too much to accommodate the two of you. It is a bright and flavorful springtime soup. They do suggest it's even better when made a day ahead and topped with a froth of champagne just before serving. I say you can start it at three in the afternoon, get in an appetite-building walk around five and eat at six. You're on your own after that—especially if you're on your own!

3 slices bacon, chopped
1 medium onion, chopped
1 large carrot, chopped
3 cups / 750 mL chicken stock
Salt to taste (depends on the saltiness of the stock)
¼-½ tsp. / 1-2 mL white pepper
½ tsp. / 2 mL dried thyme, crumbled
3 cups / 750 mL frozen baby peas, thawed and well drained
½ cup / 125 mL parsley, chopped
2 cups / 500 mL heavy cream
2 cans or corresponding amount of fresh baby clams and liquid
1 cup / 250 mL Mirassou Brut (or other dry sparkling wine)

Sauté bacon in the big soup pot until the fat is rendered. Add onion and carrot and sauté over medium heat for 5 minutes, being careful not to burn anything. Add chicken stock, salt, pepper and thyme. Cover and bring to a boil. Turn down the heat and simmer 10 minutes.

Add peas and parsley and stir. Now purée the lot in several batches in the blender or food processor to the consistency you like. Return the purée to the pot and bring to the boil one more time. As soon as it boils, take the pot off the heat and add cream and clams with their liquid. Taste and adjust seasoning as needed.

If you want to serve the soup tomorrow night, let it cool at this point and refrigerate. Just before serving, reheat carefully, stirring often. Continue heating until soup is very hot but don't let it boil again.

Just before serving the soup, stir in the sparkling wine.

Serves 4.

Accompaniment
Crisp French bread and sweet butter; focaccia, crisp crackers with Saint-André or other triple-cream cheese

Wine
Follow the first rule: whatever's in the pot can go in the glass. You did use only one cup of the bubbly!

Chilled Okanagan Apple Soup with Peppered Horseradish

Wolfgang von Wieser, *Chartwell, The Four Seasons Hotel, Vancouver*

Summer is the time for cold soups, fruit soups, wonderful bowls of garden goodies that can start a meal or be one, if you make enough and surround them with plenty of extras.

Here's a good one for a backyard barbecue: perfectly simple yet very tasty. The tang of fresh horseradish mixed with pepper and whipping cream is a unique match with the apple, cider and fresh basil.

Soup

- 2 tsp. / 10 mL sugar
- 3 Tbsp. / 40 mL sherry vinegar
- 4 Granny Smith apples, cored and quartered (you don't have to peel them if you don't want to)
- 1 2/3 cups / 400 mL apple cider
- 1 1/4 cups / 300 mL white wine
- 1/2 cinnamon stick
- 4 fresh basil leaves, julienned

Melt sugar in a heated pan until golden. Deglaze with vinegar. Add apples, apple cider, white wine, cinnamon stick. Simmer over very low heat 5 minutes. Remove from heat, cool. Strain with fine sieve. Add basil. Chill soup in individual bowls.

Garnish

- 1 tsp. / 5 mL fresh horseradish, grated
- 1/4 cup / 50 mL heavy cream, stiffly whipped
- Pinch crushed black peppercorns
- 1 Granny Smith apple, cored and sliced paper thin

Mix horseradish with whipped cream and stir in pepper. Take a cold teaspoon in each hand and form small quenelles or dumplings.

Serve soup cold and clear, with thinly sliced apples and horseradish-cream quenelles floating on top.

Serves 4.

Accompaniment
Thin slices of lightly toasted, unbuttered levain bread

Wine
Okanagan riesling, gewürztraminer

4

Memories of Jounieh: Lettuce and Tomato Soup with Lemon and Mint

I first tasted this soup in Lebanon at a splendid banquet amid all the less-than-splendidness of Beirut. It is a gorgeous, tasty, fresh-flavored soup— even if you end up using canned tomatoes as I often do because they're a lot less fussy. I suppose you could fry some good bacon and crumble it in and have a soup 'n' BLT in one. The entire enterprise shouldn't take more than half an hour and it's as easy as pie. Question: how easy is pie, really?

2 Tbsp. / 25 mL butter
2 Tbsp. / 25 mL oil
1 big onion, chopped coarsely
2 cloves garlic, chopped fine
Salt and pepper to taste (if you use canned beef stock, use very little salt)
1 big can tomatoes, chopped, with juice (or 1 quart bottle / 1 L Italian crushed tomatoes
or 2 big ripe beefsteaks, seeded and chopped)
1 cup / 250 mL hot water
2-3 cups / 500-750 mL hot beef stock (depending on how slurpy you like it)
2 packed cups / 500 mL shredded fresh romaine lettuce (or better yet, escarole; not iceberg, ever)
2/3 cup / 150 mL tiny soup pasta (orzo is about as big as you want to get)
Juice of 2 lemons

2-3 Tbsp. / 25-45 mL chopped fresh mint leaves (or 1¹/₂ tsp. / 5-7 mL dried mint, crushed in the palm of your hand)

Heat butter and oil over medium heat in a soup pot. Add onion, garlic, salt and pepper. Cook 'til onion is soft but don't let garlic burn. Mash in the tomatoes and cook 5 minutes (you want them to mush into the soup). Pour in water and broth, stir and bring to simmer. Simmer 10 minutes.

Add lettuce or escarole and cook 5 minutes more. Add pasta and cook 'til done (depending on size; 5 minutes is usually enough). Add lemon juice and mint leaves; simmer 'til everything's nicely blended, a minute or two.

Serve hot, remembering to scoop up pasta from the bottom.

For 4, if they're hungry.

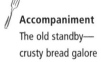

Accompaniment
The old standby—
crusty bread galore

Wine
The acid from the lemon and tomato will overpower most wines, so I wouldn't drink anything more elaborate than cool lager or even a wine cooler.

Portuguese Kale and Potato Soup (Caldo verde meu caminho)

Caldo verde *is sort of Portugal's spaghetti sauce or chili. Everybody has a slightly different recipe, another way of doing it. If you can find Portuguese olive oil, so much the better; it has a distinctive fruity green tang that gives the soup a very special flavor. A mid-size extra virgin olive oil is fine, but not one of those $25 designer models in the tall, tip-over bottle. Save that for sprinkling on fresh parmesan cheese.*

This one has worked well for me for years; sometimes I make it with a light chicken stock, if I have any, instead of water. It makes the soup richer, but purists insist on water. A key is not to mash the potatoes too fine; a few little lumps are actually desirable in this recipe. Wash the kale well in a couple of changes of cold water, rip the leafy part off the stems (throw those out) and then bunch leaves together and cut into fine, fine strips with a sharp knife.

5-6 large potatoes, peeled and cubed for cooking
Salt and ground pepper to taste
6-7 cups / 1.5-1.75 L cold water
½ cup / 25 mL olive oil
2 or 3 chouriço sausage or similar Portuguese sausage with a bit of spice
5-6 cups / 1.25-1.5 L very finely shredded kale

Boil potatoes in a big pot with the salt and water, then simmer with the lid off for 15 minutes or so. *Don't pour off the water,* but take the potatoes out with a slotted spoon and mash them in another bowl (not too fine). Beat the oil and pepper into the potatoes. Stir the mush back into the cooking water.

Meanwhile simmer the sausages, pricked 2 or 3 times with a fork, in another pot of water for about 15 minutes. Slice sausages into whatever-size pieces you like. Bring the soup to a boil again and toss in the kale. Boil for 5 to 7 minutes. Some people like the kale crunchy; not me, so I cook it longer. Add sausage slices and boil for another 2 to 3 minutes.

Serve hot or warm. Reheats magnificently. Skip the sausages and it's a fast and hearty vegetarian soup.

For a big dinner table as a first course; for 4 to 6 as a main.

Accompaniment
Portuguese buns (about a dozen for 4 diners is not excessive); marmelada, the ubiquitous Portuguese pectinated quince jam/jelly/conserve; Bel Paese cheese, en slab. I know it's not all Portuguese but I'm all in favor of extending European economic ecumenicalism to cooking.

Wine
Iced vinho verde is perfect with this, but you can also go to a light, anonymous, under-$10 Portuguese table red.

Chicken, Cheese and Cognac Soup with Capellini or Stelline (Zuppa bella Paola)

A great, tasty, practically instant soup that tastes as though you've spent hours at it. If you make it with capellini or angel hair pasta (the super-thin strands), you'll want to break it into 1- to 2-inch pieces for easier eating. That way it's angel hair with angels' share (if you use real cognac; of course cooking brandy is just fine). I've been making it more often with little pasta stars (stelline). And instead of chicken broth, a light veal stock is good too. You'll notice no salt or pepper is called for because the broth and the Gruyère are salty. Yes, a little pepper at the table if you like the taste. Otherwise it's self-contained, as listed.

I don't know who Paola was either.

6 cups / 1.5 L rich chicken broth, low
   salt
1 cup / 250 mL capellini or stelline
1 cup / 250 mL Gruyère cheese, diced or
   shredded (or ½ cup / 125 mL each
   Gruyère and Asiago)
Pepper to taste
4-5 Tbsp. / 60-75 mL cognac or brandy
1½ Tbsp. / 25 mL chopped parsley
1½ Tbsp. / 25 mL chopped sorrel
   (if there's no sorrel, double up on
   parsley)

Heat the broth to a simmer in a big pot. Add pasta and cook briefly. If using fresh capellini, 30 seconds is enough; dried, 1 to 2 minutes; stelline, 3 to 4 minutes. Stir all the time. Add cheese and continue stirring as it melts. Stir in the brandy.

Sprinkle herbs on top of each serving.

Serves 4 as a first course; 6 as a soup 'n' salad meal.

Accompaniment
Seedy buns; focaccia bread

Wine
Chilled sherry; semillon; brandy 'n' soda!

Stoertebecker Soup

Othmar Steinhart, *Fish & Co. Restaurant, Hyatt Regency Hotel, Vancouver*

This is one of those hearty north-coastal German soups that aren't much known outside north-coastal Germany. Chef Othmar let me have this after a little wheedling. Along with Bernard Plé's Kentucky Bourbon Bread Pudding (don't worry, it's in here, a few dozen pages down the way), it's the tastiest treat I've had at the Hyatt in the heart of Vancouver.

Soup

½ cup / 125 mL diced celery
½ cup / 125 mL diced onion
½ cup / 125 mL diced green pepper
½ cup / 125 mL diced red pepper
½ cup / 125 mL diced leeks
½ cup / 125 mL diced carrots
Olive oil
Fish stock

Vegetables should be cut in ¾-inch-or-so (2 cm) squares. Sauté in very hot olive oil for 3 or 4 minutes. Add a good fish stock to just cover the vegetables. Simmer for a few minutes and let cool down.

Fish

3 Tbsp. / 45 mL olive oil
1 clove garlic, crushed
Shallots, finely chopped
Fresh mussels and clams, if available
Any kind of fresh fish, cut in squares ("use whatever is local and handy: salmon, snapper, halibut . . . ")
Scallops and prawns
4 Tbsp. / 60 mL dry white wine

Heat oil, add garlic and shallots; let cook a few minutes. Add shellfish, fish, scallops. Stir. Add white wine. Put lid on pan to steam for 2 minutes. Add stock and vegetables. Mix it all up over heat.

Garnish

Salt
Pepper
Mrs. Dash
Sprinklings of saffron, fresh watercress, diced ripe tomatoes.

Season to taste. Finish off with watercress and diced tomatoes for each bowl. It all seems too simple, doesn't it.

Quantities are generic. Make what you need.

7

Accompaniment
Fresh breads, including a good, hearty sour rye

Wine
Chablis; riesling *halbtrocken*; Alsatian pinot gris; cold Beck's

BREAD

If I win the lottery and get to take the rest of my life off, I'll enroll in a serious baking course at once.

Langós

Frank Valoczy,
The Ivy Restaurant, Vancouver

Langós is the Hungarian peasant "bread" that's fried rather than baked, though up to that point it follows the conventional bread-making procedure.

I first found it in a wonderful little Vancouver restaurant called Bandi's, one of those cheerfully painted old houses that used to sit all over the downtown core of the city (and of which Bandi's and Umberto Menghi's yellow house are two of the few remaining examples).

Bandi's brought uptown Hungarian cooking to this city and most of it was due to the kitchen skills of Frank, the chef. As chefs do, he departed there quietly one day and it took a little tracking to find him again at a neighborhood place called The Ivy.

Langós should be eaten as hot as mouth and fingers can stand it, with a lot of chopped fresh garlic on top and a considerable sprinkle of sea salt. While it's a good accompaniment to various appetizers and snacks, it's best all on its own.

Don't let Frank's "may be rubbed with garlic" lull you into inaction: substitute the world "must"!

> 3½ oz. / 100 g fresh compound yeast (or 3 envelopes / 24 g dry yeast—if you use dry yeast, prepare according to package instructions)
> Pinch sugar
> 10 cups / 1½ kg all-purpose flour
> 1¼ cups / 300 mL milk at room temperature
> 5 tsp. / 30 g salt
> 4 cups / 1 L warm water
> Sunflower oil (for frying)
> Chopped garlic or garlic paste as accompaniment

Break up compound yeast into small crumbs. Combine with sugar and 1 cup (250 mL) of the flour in bowl. Pour milk over dry mixture and let stand until doubled in size. Combine remaining flour and salt, add the doubled starter and warm water.

Mix until smooth and dough no longer sticks to the side of the bowl. Cover and let stand until doubled in size.

Turn out on floured board. Roll or pat down by hand until about ¾ inch (2 cm) thick. Cut into squares or triangles about the size of your hand. Stretch each piece about an inch or two (2.5 to 5 cm) on each side (this changes the consistency of the bread). Let stand for 10 minutes.

Heat 2 inches (5 cm) sunflower oil in a saucepan until a pinch of dough will sizzle on top of the oil. Deep-fry each side until golden brown. Drain on paper towels.

May be rubbed with garlic paste, or brush on garlic processed in a blender and thinned with a little water.

Recipe should make 40 to 50 pieces.

Accompaniment
Nothing or anything!

Wine
Szekszárdi Vörös or one of those garlic-killing 15-percent alcohol reds from around Tarragona

9

Pastrami, Cheese and Sauerkraut Bread (Ready Reuben)

If I were ever to watch a Super Bowl game, I'd have to have a couple of these on hand. And some of the oven-fried lemon-parmesan potatoes (farther along in these pages). And a lot of mustards. I don't like eating cold, out-of-a-bag-or-bowl food when staring at the tube. This one worked for the time we almost got the Stanley Cup and when cousin Pat was pitching in the World Series.

2½ cups / 625 mL all-purpose flour
1 envelope / 8 g instant dry yeast
1½ Tbsp. / 25 mL sugar
1 tsp. / 5 mL salt
1 cup / 250 mL water
1½ Tbsp. / 25 mL butter
½ lb. / 250 g pastrami, shredded
¼ lb. / 125 g corned beef, shredded
½ cup / 125 mL mayonnaise
2 Tbsp. / 30 mL Dijon or other spicy mustard
1½ cups / 375 mL shredded or tiny-cubed cheese (Swiss, Gruyère, Jarlsberg, or combination)
1 cup / 250 mL very well drained sauerkraut (press it against the sides of a sieve or colander to get all the juice, otherwise it makes the bread soggy)
½ cup / 125 mL very well drained canned mushrooms
½ cup / 125 mL onions, sautéed in a little butter 'til limp
1 egg white
1 Tbsp. /15 mL water
1 Tbsp. / 15 mL caraway seeds

Mix 1½ cups (375 mL) of the flour with the yeast, sugar and salt in a big bowl. Heat the water with the butter 'til hot (103°F, 40°C). Stir hot liquid into the dry ingredients in the bowl. Start adding more of the remaining flour and mix together. Stop when you get a nice soft dough that isn't sticking to you or the bowl any more. (You might not need all of the remaining flour; it's OK.)

Cover the dough with a clean dish towel and let it rest for 10 minutes somewhere where there's no draft. Sometimes I just turn the oven on to 200°F (94°C) for 3 or 4 minutes, then shut it off and stick the bowl in there.

Grease a large baking sheet with some butter. Roll the dough onto the sheet until it's about 15 by 9 inches (38 by 23 cm). Arrange the pastrami and corned beef evenly in a stripe down the middle of the dough, leaving about 4 inches (10 cm) free at either end.

Mix the mayonnaise and the mustard together and spread on top of the meat. Sprinkle the cheese on top of the mayo-mustard. Mix the sauerkraut with the mushrooms and onions and spread that over the cheese.

Cut strips (about 1 inch / 2.5 cm

wide) from the edges of the filling to the edge of the dough. Fold both end pieces over the filling and then fold the side strips (like a braid or your sneaker laces) at an angle across the filling. You want the filling covered by dough, not completely enclosed.

Put the baking sheet over a turkey-roasting pan half full of boiling water. Put a clean towel over the bread and let it rise 30 more minutes in a warm, draft-free spot.

Beat egg white and water together with a fork and brush it on top of the bread with a pastry brush. Sprinkle caraway seeds on top.

Bake bread for 30 minutes in 400°F (200°C) oven. It should be brown on top but not too dark; you want to see some bubbling action through the slits in the top. It will most likely drip cheese and other stuff on the baking sheet, if not the oven.

Take it out, let it cool and then eat it warm or at room temperature. Leftovers go in the fridge and are great microwaved.

Makes 1 family loaf.

Accompaniment
A salad, if you feel guilty; Tim's-Cascade-style jalapeño chips otherwise

Wine
Château d'Yquem spritzers; quart of Labatt's 50; Bowen Island Blonde Ale

12

Pithiviers with Ham and Chard

Mirassou Vineyards, San Jose, California

Pithiviers is a pastry tart, often filled with almond cream, and named after the French town in the South of France. Filling it with ham, chard and cheese makes it a wonderful brunch number. You can make it ahead and serve it either warm or cold. It's another of a sizeable handful of recipes created or commissioned by the Mirassou family of winemakers who continue to create one of the tastiest Petite Sirahs in all of California. Not that I'd serve that with this . . .

Accompaniment
A little fresh garden salad with a gentle dressing and the world's a better place already.

Wine
Mirassou Chardonnay or Petite Rosé

1 bunch red or green Swiss chard, cleaned and deribbed
½ lb. (1½ cups) / 250 g diced cooked ham
½ cup / 125 g crumbled good 'n' tangy goat cheese
3 whole green onions, finely sliced
¼ tsp. / 1 mL salt
¼ tsp. / 1 mL pepper, freshly ground
3 large eggs (reserve one for pastry-wash)
1¼ lbs. / 625 g puff pastry
(or 1 pkg. frozen puff pastry sheets; those Pepperidge Farms numbers work pretty well)

Steam the chard, minus ribs, until tender. Cool and squeeze dry. Aim for about 1 cup (250 mL) finished chard. Chop very fine and combine with ham, cheese, green onions, salt and pepper and 2 beaten eggs and mix well.

Roll out the pastry to ¼ inch (5 mm) thick (pre-rolled sheets are a lot easier to handle), and cut out 2 pastry circles, each 9 inches (23 cm) in diameter. Place one on a cookie sheet and spread filling evenly in the middle, leaving about 1 inch (2.5 cm) uncovered all around. Brush uncovered part with the remaining egg-wash. Top with the other circle and seal all around.

Using the blunt side of a knife, pull the pastry edge in about ½ inch (1.5 cm) at 1-inch (2.5 cm) intervals, to create a scalloped edge. Brush the tart with more beaten egg. Cut a small vent hole in the middle and with a knife point, make a spiral from the edges to the center, cutting about a quarter-way into the dough.

Refrigerate the assembled tart for a couple of hours or longer. Bake at 375°F (190°C) for 30 minutes until puffed and golden brown. Cool and slice into servings.

Serves 6.

Convict Bread (Pain bagnard)

Robert Le Crom, *Hotel Vancouver*

"Convict's bread," eh? If this is what Jean Valjean was tucking into (Robert Le Crom reminded me of Victor Hugo as he urged me to tuck in), maybe the show ought to be known as Les Not-All-That-Bad-Actually!

This spicy party bread is even better than the one you hollow out and fill up with cream cheese and spinach, or the one with the Italian sausage and provolone baked in a big round Italian loaf. It's a big wheel of bread stuffed with a hot (as in spicy) and cheesy filling.

I made it for every World Series, Stanley Cup, poker game, bridal shower, kids' sleep-over and cat show on the calendar for a year.

Best when served immediately after it's done, according to the chef. Take two, they're big.

Bread

Two loaves' worth of your favorite bread dough recipe (add some rye flour and a few hot pimentos to give it some body). Bake in galette style: large, round, low pans about 4 inches (10 cm) deep, 15 inches (37 cm) in diameter. Cut galettes in half horizontally. Sprinkle top and bottom with olive oil and pesto, to taste.

Filling

- 2 medium onions, sliced
- 2 red peppers, sliced
- 2 green peppers, sliced
- 20 kalamata olives, coarsely chopped
- 20 green olives, coarsely chopped
- 6 garlic cloves, coarsely chopped
- Olive oil
- Oregano and rosemary
- Fresh goat cheese
- Fresh herbs for garnish

Sauté onions, peppers, olives and garlic in olive oil with oregano and rosemary until tender. Spread mixture on bottom half of galette. Sprinkle with fresh goat cheese to taste. Replace top half of galette and press firmly together. (If there's too much filling, serve it tomorrow as a side dish.)

Bake at 375° (190°C) for 10 to 15 minutes until cheese melts slightly. Remove from oven and place on large platter. Cut into pie-shaped wedges. Insert a skewer into middle of each wedge to secure. Border the platter with more fresh herbs—rosemary, basil, thyme.

Serves 6 or 8.

13

Accompaniment
A hearty green salad (not too fussy with edible flowers, thanks!)

Wine
Red and raunchy; beer's even better.

14

Wild Rice, Corn and Oatmeal Bread

Anja Vogels, *Sardis*

For a while there Otto Bjornson would arrive once a week, Monday mornings, usually even earlier than the paper.

He'd pull into the drive in his boxy, beige, cool van. Depending on the instructions that had been placed in the plastic bag and twist-tied to the front door handle the night before, Otto would start stacking stuff on the step.

Otto was one of the last of the peripatetic milkmen—pretty much a vanished breed in most places now. Orange juice or cookie dough, yogurt or eggs, wild rice—Otto left lots of things besides milk—coupons, recipes, samples, offers, suggestions, just plain common sense too. If it looked as if it might be a sunny day, Otto stashed the cartons and containers somewhere shady.

If he got an order mixed up—it happened once or twice, though most likely the mixing was on my part, when the order forms started looking like tax returns with all those lines and boxes—he left a little "apology": a quart of juice, a brace of chocolate milk packs, a tub of cottage cheese.

One of the best things he ever left on the doorstep was a small bag of wild rice. It came with a lime-neon sheet of paper headed "Rise 'N Shine." In the bag were a couple of grams of Zizania

aquatica—the seeds of an annual watergrass that isn't really rice at all. The Chippewa Indians called it "good berry," a special gift from the Creator to keep them fit and strong.

Shortly afterwards, Otto went off to promote his wild rice full time. We still call it Otto's bread at our house, even though it's Anja Vogels's recipe. Toasted, it's even better.

> 2 pkg. / 16 g or 2 Tbsp. / 25 mL yeast
> Pinch sugar
> 1/2 cup / 125 mL warm water
> 2 cups / 500 mL warm milk
> 1/2 cup / 125 mL pure maple syrup
> 4 Tbsp. / 60 mL unsalted butter, melted
> 5 to 5 1/2 cups / 1.25-1.5 L unbleached flour
> 1 Tbsp. / 15 mL salt
> 1 cup / 250 mL wild rice, cooked
> 1/2 cup / 125 mL cornmeal
> 1 1/2 cups / 375 mL large-flake rolled oats
> 1 Tbsp. / 15 mL flour, for sprinkling
> 2 Tbsp. / 30 mL oatmeal, for sprinkling
> 2 Tbsp. / 30 mL cornmeal, for sprinkling

In a small bowl sprinkle yeast and sugar over warm water. Stir to dissolve and let stand until foamy, about 10 minutes.

In a big mixing bowl combine milk, maple syrup and butter. Add 1 cup flour, salt, wild rice, cornmeal and oats. Beat until smooth, about 1 minute. Add yeast mixture and 1/2 cup (125 mL) more flour. Beat for 2 minutes. With a wooden spoon continue to beat in remaining flour,

½ cup (125 mL) at a time until a soft dough is formed, just clearing the side of the bowl.

Turn dough out on a lightly floured surface. Knead until smooth and springy, about 5 minutes, adding 1 Tbsp. (15 mL) of flour at a time as necessary to prevent sticking. The dough will have a delicate, tacky yet "nubby" quality.

Place in deep, greased container. Turn once to coat the top and cover bowl with plastic wrap. Let rise at room temperature for an hour or so until doubled in bulk.

Turn dough out onto work surface and divide into 3 equal portions. Form each portion into a round loaf. Place on a very large greased baking sheet sprinkled with a mixture of flour, oatmeal and cornmeal. Roll the tops of the loaves in the mixture to coat lightly. Cover loosely with plastic wrap and let rise at room temperature until doubled in bulk again, about 45 minutes.

With a serrated knife, slash a cross on top of each loaf, no deeper than ¼ inch (5 mm). Bake at 375°F (190°C) for 30 to 35 minutes until brown (loaves will sound hollow when tapped). Cool on a rack before slicing.

Makes 3 loaves.

Accompaniment
Lots of butter, jam, marmalade, syrup, double cream— anything rich, sweet, suspect

Wine
Ovaltine? Coffee? English Breakfast tea?

16

Walnut Bread

Renee Carisio,
Trefethen Vineyards, Napa, California

The taste of warm fresh bread with savory walnuts—not just any old walnuts, but the ones that grow between the grapevines at Trefethen Vineyards in the Napa Valley—a grand treat.

One of my best wine-country memories is a short stay at the Trefethen guesthouse: waking up in the morning in the middle of a working vineyard with the sound of birds and sprinklers going, lumbering old trucks out on Highway 29 hauling crates of cuttings up the slope—and the secure knowledge there was a nice little breakfast chardonnay in the cooler!

The walnuts arrived unannounced one day in the mail in a linen bag with a couple of recipes attached and the lyrics to the Trefethen Walnuts' song, which runs to the tune of "I Heard It Through the Grapevine" ("Ooo-ooh, we grew between the grapevines . . ." etc.)

I don't know if it's the proximity of the cabernet that makes the walnuts so tasty or the influence of the walnuts that ameliorates the wine, but I wouldn't change a thing.

Accompaniment
Nothing's better than sweet butter—maybe Jersey double cream.

Wine
Light and red—Trefethen's own Eshcol is ideal.

1 Tbsp. / 15 mL yeast
5 Tbsp. / 75 mL honey
1½ cups / 375 mL warm water
2 cups / 500 mL toasted walnuts
4 Tbsp. / 60 mL extra virgin olive oil
2 tsp. / 10 mL kosher salt
4 cups / 1 L unbleached flour

Dissolve yeast and honey in warm water. Grind walnuts in food processor until very fine and a paste begins to form on the bottom of the bowl. Combine dissolved yeast, 2 Tbsp. (30 mL) of the olive oil and salt in the bowl of heavy-duty mixer. Add 3 cups (750 mL) of the flour. Beat 2 minutes until smooth. Add walnuts. Gradually add remaining flour. Beat approximately 5 minutes.

Transfer to lightly floured board. Knead briefly (dough will be slightly tacky). Place in bowl oiled with remaining 2 Tbsp. (30 mL) olive oil and cover with a towel. Let rise until dough doubles in size (about 1½ to 2 hours). Punch down and shape into 3 or 4 round loaves. Let rise 30 minutes.

Bake on a preheated baking stone in a preheated 400°F (200°C) oven for 40 minutes.

Makes 3 to 4 loaves.

PASTA

Pasta
is probably what
I eat most of.

18

Pappardelle with Fiddleheads and Bocconcini

Alan Groom, *Bacchus Ristorante, the Wedgewood Hotel, Vancouver*

Alan Groom is one of the new breed of British chefs. There was a time when chefs were all named André or Michel or Pierre, occasionally Karlheinz, now and then Giovanni. Now there are many with English names, all over the map. I do wonder what it is about Yorkshire that turns out so many great ones: Michael Quinn, Brian Turner—and here in Vancouver and here to stay, it appears, Alan Groom.

The man can cook anything, which is after all the sign of a great chef. His hand is particularly dab with seafood (any time there's a sea bass to be had by his hand, order it!) and he's happy as a clam with the gently Italian style of cuisine at the best-kept-secret kind of place he oversees in downtown Vancouver.

In fact, this pasta was an all-but-unlisted accompaniment to one of his fabulous fishes—so simple, deft, delicate I had to have it in a permanent file. After a bit of badgering the chef came up with this serves-two version, which I've polished a little to please my own palate. Does the trick for guests, two or twenty, too.

Accompaniment
Baguette, seedy buns

Wine
Cool Beaujolais, robust semillon

Olive oil for sautéing
2 oz. / 60 g pancetta, diced
2 Tbsp. / 30 mL chopped onion
1 tsp. / 5 mL fresh sage, chopped
1 Tbsp. / 15 mL lemon juice
1 Tbsp. / 15 mL chicken stock
1 Tbsp. / 15 mL extra virgin olive oil
6 slices bocconcini
Handful fiddleheads, blanched
Fresh pappardelle pasta, cooked for 1-2
    minutes

Sauté pancetta and onion in a little oil. Add sage, lemon juice, chicken stock and the 1 Tbsp. (15 mL) oil and reduce until slightly thickened. Add blanched fiddleheads, heat through. Add fresh-cooked pasta. Coat with sauce. Add bocconcini at the last minute.

Serves 2.

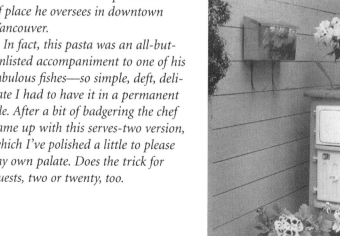

Miss C's Chicken Soup, Turkey Wiener, Peas and Spinach Pasta Jumble

There was a time not long ago when the Child of the House was stuck in her beige-food mode—if it had any other color on or about it, it was infra dig. Pasta, dead-plain, unsauced, unseasoned, with a sprinkle of parmesan and no butter. The Cat of the House was in agreement and the two of them spent happy hours sharing dinner.

Periodically, I would attempt to . . . not so much push the envelope as try to finesse it a little. Most of the time the ploy was seen through. Once in a while it worked. This is one of those onces: a little green from the peas and spinach, a little pink from the turkey wieners and so on. Not exactly Jackson Pollock on the plate, but still, edging along the palette, gently nudging the bounds and bond of beigeness.

Good noodles and a lot of cream always bring out the poet in me!

½ lb. / 250 g medium pasta shells, bows, squiggles, favorite pasta, cooked al dente and drained

1 small pkg. frozen peas, thawed and drained

1 small pkg. frozen spinach, thawed

3 Tbsp. / 45 mL melted butter

1 lb. / 500 g turkey wieners, sliced ½" (1.5 cm) thick

1 can cream of chicken soup

½ cup / 125 mL sour cream

½ cup / 125 mL whole milk

Salt and pepper as (and if!) you like it

6 thick slices bacon, cooked and diced or crumbled, fat drained off

In a big bowl stir up cooked pasta, half of the peas and the melted butter. Fiercely. Butter a big flat baking dish and cover the bottom with the spinach. Put pasta and pea mixture on top.

Mix the turkey wieners, cream of chicken soup, sour cream and milk thoroughly in another bowl (might as well use the one the pasta and peas just came out of). Pour over pasta. Bake uncovered in 400°F (200°C) oven for 20 minutes.

Sprinkle the rest of the peas and the bacon on top and bake another 8 to 10 minutes until it's bubbling a bit and there are some brown pasta bits sticking out. I like the crusty-baked parts best so I use the largest, flattest baking dish in the kitchen.

Let sit for a few minutes before serving.

For 4 to 6, depending on appetites.

Accompaniment

Carrot sticks, celery, broccoli, sliced tomato, avocado (if the mother of the house is at home; chocolate chip cookies if she's not).

Wine

Yop! All right, a little edelzwicker from Alsace for me.

Spaghettini à la Skippy

Sharon Wildwind, *Calgary*

The things I've asked my long-suffering DiscDrive *listeners to come up with for me! Limericks with improbable words in them, newel-post being the most benign in one contest. Names of obscure movie stars which have flown from my memory. Persimmon and chestnut-flour recipes. The Sanskrit word for salad bar. A Lamborghini.*

They've come through in all those but one, though, in fairness, the same person who supplied this recipe did send a Lamborghini. It was a little small to accommodate me comfortably but it makes a nice desk-toy; and another listener sent a photo of his all-wooden version, which he called a Lumberghini.

One afternoon, driving the discs and musing as always, I was struck by the fact that the only foods currently popular at my home among the under-ten population were avocado, cottage cheese, peanut butter, spaghetti and chicken soup.

Could, I wondered out loud, someone combine all those into a recipe that would actually be edible? Someone could; in fact several someones sent in their versions. Dutifully I cooked them all and this worked best. In fact, it's very good. And it's led me to a pleasant all-by-phone friendship with its author as we chatted our way

through various milestones in our respective lives from weddings to book publishings and wine dinners.

Now I'm wondering, what can you do with dried pears, chicken liver, kasha, kohlrabi, marzipan and oysters . . .

4 Tbsp. / 60 mL unsalted butter, cut in bits
2 Tbsp. / 30 mL onions, finely chopped
4 Tbsp. / 60 mL celery, finely chopped
1 Tbsp. / 15 mL flour
1 cup / 250 mL chicken stock
Sufficient spaghettini to serve 2
½ cup / 125 mL crunchy peanut butter at room temperature
Salt
Lemon juice
Garlic (optional)
1 Tbsp. / 15 mL parsley
1 cup / 250 mL cottage cheese at room temperature
1 ripe avocado, sliced
Roasted peanuts, ground

Melt half the butter in a pan. Sauté onions and celery. Mix in flour and cook briefly, then add chicken stock. Stir constantly with a whisk, bringing to a boil over high heat until mixture thickens. Simmer until vegetables are semi-mushy. Meanwhile put spaghettini on to cook.

When vegetable-stock mixture is cooked, press it through a sieve with the back of a spoon, then return to the stock. If you'd rather have vegetables chunky, cook them a little less and don't bother with this step. Put peanut butter in a large mixing bowl and whisk in stock until you like the consistency. You may not need all the stock, especially if you like thicker pasta sauce. Return mixture to the pot. Add salt and lemon juice. Simmer over moderate heat, don't boil. Set aside.

Melt remaining butter. Sauté garlic and parsley. When spaghettini is cooked, drain well, then coat with garlic and parsley.

Layer the ingredients on a warmed platter: spaghettini first, then spoon cottage cheese over it and pour warm peanut sauce over all.

Garnish with slices of a not-over-ripe avocado. Sprinkle ground roasted peanuts over everything.

For 2.

Accompaniment
Tomato, red onion and bocconcini salad

Wine
White zinfandel at the elder end of the table; cranberry-raspberry drink at the younger

22

Untitled (Radiatore in a Rush)

The reason this is titled Untitled is that I didn't have time to give it a name and anyway, I've always liked the sense of artistic mystery that goes with the term. It's like looking at the canvas and thinking, I don't know what to call this. So I threw everything in the pot (I was in a rush), looked in and saw pepper and garlic, the surprise of new potatoes, broccoli, pumpkin seeds, and then the pasta and thought, well, I could call this pasta with pepper, garlic, potatoes, broccoli and pumpkin seeds. The acronym would have been clumsy—Pasta PGPBPS (though, if you get a ⁵⁄₄ rhythm going it's finger-snapping like so: Pea-gee-pea-bee-pea-s).

As with many good recipes, it was at least halfway through the making before I realized it was going to be pretty good and worth keeping. That's the point at which you have to backtrack to remember what's gone in so far. Feel free to add or subtract anything. Feel free to give it a name while you're at it.

Accompaniment
Cold sliced smoked-turkey breast; slabs of Mennonite summer sausage; broiled halibut

Wine
Montepulciano in a screwtop

3 cups new potatoes, cubed and cooked
2 cups / 500 mL pasta shapes (radiatore, fusilli), cooked al dente
3 cups / 750 mL broccoli tops
¼ - ½ cup / 50-125 mL pumpkin seeds, lightly toasted
Olive oil for sautéing
1 medium red pepper, julienned
½ tsp. / 2 mL dried hot red pepper flakes
1 small garlic clove, slivered
2 Tbsp. / 30 mL extra virgin olive oil
Asiago cheese, grated
Sea salt to taste
Parsley, chopped

Cook potatoes; keep warm. Cook pasta; keep warm. Blanch broccoli; keep warm. Toast pumpkin seeds (dry, no oil) in oven.

Heat olive oil in a large pan. Add strips of red pepper and pepper flakes and sauté 2 to 3 minutes. Add garlic and sauté 1 minute more.

In a big bowl, toss pasta with extra virgin olive oil and cheese. Add potatoes and pumpkin seeds, mix well. Add broccoli and mix some more. Pour over red pepper, pepper flakes and garlic in oil, toss well. Sprinkle sea salt and parsley on top.

For 4.

Concorde Penne

The one and only time I flew on the Concorde they weren't serving pasta but if they ever decide to, this is the sort of dish I'd hope for. In fact, come to think of it, I wasn't big-time impressed with the food. I mean the wines were wonderful and the plane landed at Heathrow while I still had my cognac glass half full—didn't spill any, either!—and the thought of making the trip in 3 hours and 17 minutes according to my Shoppers Drug Mart Timex was impressive. But for food they (perhaps wisely) served all that stuff that's not so much a mark of any chef's skills as Mother Nature's: caviar, chilled lobster, etc. Nice, but I'd have loved a bit of stew, maybe. If CP Air had ever got a Concorde when Olympian chef Bruno Marti was in charge of catering, he'd have done that—as he did his crockpot cuisine between Vancouver and San Francisco—wonderful memories of in-flight eating, that.

This is an unrepentant carnivore's dish, I'm afraid: rich, robust and reheatable enough for company the next day, so make lots.

4 slices bacon (gammon, if you can
    find it)
½ lb. / 250 g beef filet, sliced
2 Tbsp. / 25 mL flour
2 Tbsp. / 25 mL olive oil
½ lb. / 250 g turkey breast, sliced
Salt and white pepper to taste

½ cup / 125 mL white wine
1 cup / 250 mL rich chicken stock, hot
1 lb. / 500 g penne pasta or fusilli
    or macaroni
6 Tbsp. / 90 mL unsalted butter
1 cup / 250 mL freshly grated parmesan
    cheese
Handful of favorite fresh garden herbs

Put the bacon in a big pot. Dredge the beef in a little flour and brown it in the oil in a frying pan. Place beef slices on top of the bacon in the pot. Brown the turkey slices in the same pan and oil as the beef was browned, and place turkey on top of the beef. Add salt and pepper. Pour in white wine and cook over medium for a few minutes. Pour in the hot chicken stock and cook for 20 minutes over medium-low heat.

Meanwhile, cook pasta in lots of salted water to your favorite degree of *dente*-ness. Drain and put pasta in a heated bowl. Add butter in dabs and mix in well.

Remove meat from pan, sprinkle with herbs and keep warm. Pour the meat-wine sauce over the pasta and mix together with the cheese.

Place pasta on individual plates, arrange slices of meat on or around pasta, and have more parmesan on hand.

Serves 4.

Accompaniment
Some simply steamed vegetables on the side; lots of bread for sopping the sauce. (The meat makes great focaccia-and-bocconcini sandwiches if there's any left over in the morning.)

Wine
Domaine Oriental Sauvignon/Semillon, from Chile; Georges Duboeuf Fleurie, from France; Domaine de Chaberton Pinot Noir, from Langley

24

Pasta Aromatico (Fettuccine Old Krupnik)

This pasta with a bewilderment of fresh herbs is almost a Christmas dish, it smells so like holiday baking. Where else can you get your noodles with sage and cloves and nutmeg—short of Scarborough Fair? The basis for this comes from an anonymous cookbook I bought at a car wash decades ago. Now that I've made it forty or fifty times it bears the unmistakable stamp of wild-eyed creativity. It gets more creative by the minute and rewards liberal ingesting of wine while working. The success of the taste is due to the fresh herbs.

Accompaniment

Caesar salad, garlic

Wine

Sumac Ridge
Private Reserve
Gewürztraminer;
DeRham Bardolino
Chiaretto

6 slices lean bacon, chopped
2 medium onions, chopped
6 Tbsp. / 90 mL olive oil
1½ Tbsp. / 25 mL flour
8-10 rosemary leaves (if the strong
    flavor doesn't agree with you use 3-4
    Tbsp. / 45-60 mL chopped parsley
    instead, or in addition)
3 medium bay leaves, fresh if possible
3 large fresh sage leaves
4 whole cloves
6-8 medium tomatoes, cut in pieces
    (peeled if you feel like it, but who's
    going to notice, really?)
Salt and pepper as required
½ cup / 125 mL strong chicken broth,
    hot
3 cloves garlic

8 fresh basil leaves
Smidge nutmeg
3 Tbsp. / 45 mL unsalted butter
1 cup / 250 mL fresh parmesan, grated
1½ lb. / 750 g fettuccine

Sauté bacon and onion in oil 'til golden. Pour off some of the fat if there's a lot, but don't lose it all. Stir in flour and cook briefly; add rosemary if you're using it, bay leaves, sage and cloves and mix up. Add tomatoes, salt and pepper, hot chicken broth, stir well and simmer 30 minutes.

Meanwhile, crush garlic on a chopping board and chop fine together with basil and parsley, if you're using it. Sprinkle nutmeg on top of the mix and work in. Add butter, a pinch of pepper and 2 Tbsp. (30 mL) of parmesan to the mixture. Smash it all into a paste with a spoon or spatula.

When sauce has cooked 30 minutes let it cool a bit, remove bay leaves and put sauce into a blender to make it smooth. Return sauce to the cooking pan, add garlic paste and bring all to a boil again. Hold on low simmer.

Meanwhile, cook and drain the pasta and put it into a big hot serving bowl. Pour on sauce and half the cheese, mixing well. Top individual servings with more cheese.

Serves 6, before the main course.

Spaghetti Pie (Frittata) with Major Onions

There have been a dozen or more spaghetti frittata recipes that have come my way. This one combines the best parts of most.

I think my favorite ever was eaten in New Zealand for breakfast at a jolly little B&B. This dish works just as well cool and can go for school lunch or next-day-snack. While all those onions give it the heartiness I like, kids seem to prefer it without the onions, hence the call for carrots.

I'm not being facetious about the Beaujolais Nouveau reference. The most important thing to remember about the young November wine is to eat something, anything, while you're quaffing away; otherwise you'll have to call the pile-driving company in the morning and book off sick.

½ lb. / 250 g spaghetti, cooked al dente, drained and rinsed
2 Tbsp. / 25 mL unsalted butter
2 Tbsp. / 25 mL olive oil
¼ cup / 50 mL red onion, chopped
¼ cup / 50 mL white onion, chopped
1 clove garlic, chopped
¼ cup / 50 mL green onion, chopped
4-5 eggs, beaten
½ cup / 125 mL shredded parmesan
Chopped parsley
Salt and white pepper to taste
¼ cup / 50 mL shredded aged cheddar

Heat butter and oil together in a big pan. Add red and white onions and cook 5 minutes. Add garlic and green onions and cook 2 minutes.

Beat eggs well and add all onions and garlic. Add parmesan, parsley, salt and pepper. Mix well and add cooked spaghetti. Butter a pie pan large enough to accommodate everything. Press mixture into the pan.

Bake in center of 350°F (180°C) oven for 20 to 25 minutes, bring it out, sprinkle on the cheddar and bake for 5 to 10 minutes more, until the cheddar melts and bubbles. Let cool a little, cut in wedges and serve.

Plain, unsauced leftover spaghetti can be used for this. If you're making it for kids, leave out the onions and the garlic and instead, sauté 1½ (375 mL) cups shredded carrots in butter and use in place of onions.

Serves 4 to 6.

Accompaniment
Big green salad with tomato wedges

Wine
Beaujolais Nouveau

26

Angel Hair Pasta with Pecans and Asparagus

Pecans are my favorite nuts for combining with other foods, especially in pasta dishes and desserts. They're not bad just by the handful out of a bag either. Periodically Mrs. Brown, who toils with me in this vale of tears from time to time, goes south to where there seem to be major pecan forests, from which she will return with a big bag full. On those occasions I dig out all the recipes I can and make everything as quickly as possible. This is one of those favorite foods.
P.S. I say pea-CAN, not p'CAWN. How about you?

Accompaniment

Simple sprouty salad:
1 small Napa cabbage, shredded;
chopped sunflower sprouts, sorrel and arugula, handful of chopped fresh tarragon, walnut oil and vinegar dressing

Wine

Jackson-Triggs Okanagan Dry Riesling

½ cup / 125 mL pea-CAN halves
6 Tbsp. / 90 mL soft unsalted butter
2 Tbsp. / 30 mL shallots, chopped fine
10-12 thin asparagus spears, trimmed, pared and cut into ½" / 1.5 cm diagonals
¾ lb. / 350 g fresh angel hair pasta (a bit less if it's dried)

Toast pecans for about 10 to 12 minutes at 350°F (180°C), all nicely spread out on a cookie sheet. Grind in a mortar (or mechanically) and make a paste with the nuts and 5 Tbsp. (75 mL) of the butter.

Heat remaining butter in a small skillet. Add shallots and sauté for 3 minutes. Add asparagus and stir. Cover skillet and cook 3 to 4 minutes.

Meanwhile cook pasta briefly, 2 to 4 minutes, drain and keep hot. Add asparagus and butter, tossing well. Put pecan paste on top and mix well.

Serves 4.

FISH

Here we are surrounded by
water and all that dwells therein,
and how many of us ever
get past the smoked salmon?

28

Steamed Pomelo Peel Stuffed with Shrimp Purée

Kam Shing Lam, *Grand King Seafood Restaurant, Vancouver*

Don't let the innocuous name mislead you; this is elaborate, time-consuming and fussy. Oh, cooking the thing won't take long—it's the prep for the pomelo. These are the big grapefruity looking things with the spongy peel. That's the prized part. In the little back street restaurants of Martinique it's conserve de chadec: sweet, tangy, rich and dark, as dramatic in flavor as it is uninspired in appearance.

Chef Lam has created a magnificent dish that calls for prepared pomelo in a sauce based on egg white, with puréed prawns and barely-set egg yolk on top, steamed sweet-and-bitter greens on the side. Alas, it takes days to do. There are twenty-something steps involved. If you need a kitchen challenge, by all means go to it.

A much easier way to enjoy it, of course, is to call the Grand King and ask maître d' Simon Lee if it's on the menu. But some people do like an Everest and this is easily the most complicated recipe in this, or nearly any, book.

Accompaniment
Rice; steamed noodles

Wine
White peony tea

Any number of 1 lb. / ½ kg pomelos (the weight means maximum tenderness of peel and pith). Frozen peel is occasionally found in Chinese markets.
Water
1 fresh rock cod
Oil for frying
Dried shrimp
Ginger
Garlic
Water to cover

Boil peel in water 5 minutes. Rinse under cold water until cool to touch. Squeeze out as much water as possible. Soak in cold water again until it's absorbed water.

Then boil, rinse, squeeze and soak three more times.

Store peel in cold water overnight.

Repeat the boiling, rinsing, squeezing and soaking procedure three more times.

Test peel for bitterness by biting into the fleshiest part. If still bitter, repeat b-r-s-s procedure as often as needed until no bitterness remains.

Clean and scale a fresh rock cod and cut into chunks. Pan-fry fish pieces in a wok with oil until golden. Add a little more oil, dried shrimp, ginger, garlic and water to the wok. Reduce heat and simmer 1 hour or until volume is reduced by half.

Dip peel into an oil well and saturate each piece. Lay pieces of peel on bamboo dividers. Stack dividers in soup pot. Pour in reduced broth and add water if needed to make sure all peel is submerged.

Weigh down the peel and dividers with a bowl of water so they do not break apart while cooking. Cook peel over low heat for 2 hours, maintaining a steady simmer, adding water as needed to keep peel submerged.

Remove each peel carefully. It should be firm but tender. Store in freezer until you intend to use.

Later, that same year . . .

Prepared peel of ½ pomelo
Flour for dusting
½ lb. / 250 g fresh prawn meat, puréed
1 set egg yolk, salted
½ cup / 125 mL chicken broth
½ Tbsp. / 8 mL cornstarch mixed with
 3 Tbsp. / 45 mL cold water
Salt and pepper to taste
1 egg white, lightly whipped

Trim prepared pomelo peel into 8 small squares with a spoon. Dig out a small space in the middle of each square. Lightly coat indentation with all-purpose flour. Stuff prawn purée into the center. Flatten to a dome-shaped cap on top of the peel. Flatten salted egg yolk with a cleaver. Cut yolk into 8 diamond shapes. Arrange egg on top of prawn purée.

Steam stuffed peel squares over high heat 5 minutes. Meanwhile, bring chicken broth to boil and add cornstarch solution. Bring to a boil again, stirring continuously to thicken broth into a sauce. Season with salt and pepper to taste. Remove from heat and add egg white while stirring constantly, breaking up the egg. Pour over peel squares and serve with sautéed mustard greens and Chinese broccoli.

It is safe to say that if you serve this at a party it will be (A) the most unusual dish on the table; and (B) a long time coming. Does beat your cousin Brenda's hollowed-out sourdough loaf with the spinach and sour cream, though.

Rewards 4 patient souls.

30

Ken's Same Old Ahi Tuna

Ken Bogas, *Mangiamo! Vancouver*

It's a wonder this recipe is here at all. But, swears Ken Bogas, "this recipe is the only constant in my life!"

It's been on the menu of each of his last three restaurants and it's on again at his new fourth one in Vancouver's Yaletown. At the time I asked him for it he was in the middle of construction. But there was precedent. Gourmet magazine had already asked for it so he didn't have to reconstruct it completely from memory.

As I am writing this, that new restaurant has been open just one night. It's a quarter after seven in the morning and I'll give Ken another twenty minutes, half an hour, before I phone him at home to see how it all went.

Ken is one of the great fish cooks, not only in this region but anywhere. He is to the West Coast what the chef at Le Bernardin is to New York.

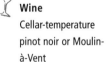

Accompaniment
Plain pasta or lightly scented rice; grilled new potatoes brushed with oil

Wine
Cellar-temperature pinot noir or Moulin-à-Vent

4 6-oz. / 170 g fresh ahi tuna steaks each ¾" / 2 cm thick
Sunflower oil
3 tsp. / 15 mL minced fresh dill
Black pepper, cracked
6 Tbsp. / 90 mL butter
3 green onions, finely sliced
1 tsp. / 5 mL minced fresh cilantro
1½ Tbsp. / 25 mL fresh lime juice
1½ Tbsp. / 25 mL Japanese soy sauce
1-1½ Tbsp. / 15-25 mL prepared wasabi
Tobiko (Japanese flying fish roe), optional

Brush tuna with oil and sprinkle with dill and pepper. Assemble sauce ingredients in small saucepan. Heat grill to high. Place tuna 4 inches (10 cm) below grill and sear for 2 minutes. Rotate 90 degrees and turn; turn again after 60 seconds. Remove from grill while tuna is still rare.

Combine other ingredients and heat slowly, stirring constantly until sauce thickens slightly, and pour over tuna.

"Throw tobiko at plate from about 3 feet away, creating a lovely Jackson Pollock effect."

Serves 4.

Grilled Salmon with Rum and Brown Sugar

Dan Atkinson,
Salmon House on the Hill, West Vancouver

Dan Atkinson is the kingpin (or is it kingfish?) of salmon cooks in these parts. Head Guy is what I mean. Presiding over the smoking alder grills at a spectacular view-spot halfway up a major mountain, he's put the lie to the old saw that a great view and good food are mutually exclusive.

While salmon is the restaurant's mainstay, Dan cooks his way beautifully through any kind of cuisine—fish or fowl, meat or vegetables. His secrets seem to be simple ones: green alder for hot, long-burning and fragrant coals. Fresh-as-can-be salmon, wild or farmed (Salmon House runs an annual promotion that gives diners the choice of sampling both side by side; the preference is pretty evenly split). Not-too-elaborate seasonings and a splash of something spirited, in this case rum, me hearties.

Just make sure the barbecue's operational before you begin making this dish. Get started five to six hours before dinner.

8 escalopes of salmon, about
  3 oz. / 85 g each
1/2 cup / 125 mL white sugar
1/2 cup / 125 mL demerara sugar
1/4 cup / 50 mL salt
1/4 cup / 50 mL fresh dill, minced
1 tsp. / 5 mL black peppercorns, cracked
1/2 cup / 125 mL Jamaican rum

Mix all dry ingredients in a food processor until well combined and granular. Season salmon liberally with the dry mixture. Sprinkle rum over the fish. Cover and chill 4 hours.

Pour off excess liquid. Heat and oil a grill (preferably over alder wood). Place salmon on hot grill and sear for 2 to 3 minutes per side.

Serves 4.

Accompaniment
Chilled fresh fruit salsa; tiny boiled potatoes or fluffy rice; something crisp and green and something red, vegetable-wise

Wine
Hainle Vineyards Estate Dry Traminer or Sumac Ridge Private Reserve Gewürztraminer from B.C.; Monterey Vineyards Chardonnay from California

32

Trout and Shrimp Hash

Kerry Sear,
The Four Seasons Olympic Hotel, Seattle

There's some reason to think it was Kerry Sear who really rocked the boat and set my home town on its ear when he came here fresh from England to galvanize the Chartwell kitchen in The Four Seasons Hotel.

When Seattle's venerable Olympic lured him away I was convinced we'd never find his equal. Of course there have been some splendid chefs at the Four Seasons since, several of them having contributed recipes to this collection. And Kerry shows no sign of either flaming out or wanting to depart Seattle, but just goes from strength to strength with glorious cuisine. With Fullers's Monique Barbeau and Tom Douglas of Etta's Seafood, Sear completes the triumvirate of top Seattle cooks, for my money.

He whipped this up for a brunch that also offered a roulade of Chinese greens, herbs and black walnuts, a "cake" of caviar and smoked salmon in a lemon-chive sauce, and sand-shark with mushroom fritters in a red wine sauce.

You can visit The Four Seasons Olympic in Seattle and try to arm-wrestle those others out of him. You'll eat well in the process.

This is a dazzling Sunday brunch dish.

Accompaniment
Crusty country bread

Wine
Blue Mountain
Okanagan Brut;
pinot blanc

½ cup / 125 mL savoy cabbage, shredded
1 Tbsp. / 15 mL sliced onion
2 Tbsp. / 30 mL butter, for cooking
2 Tbsp. / 30 mL diced cooked potato
2 Tbsp. / 30 mL flaked smoked trout
2 Tbsp. / 30 mL baby shrimp
Salt and pepper
1 egg, poached
2 Tbsp. / 30 mL wilted spinach
1 tsp. / 5 mL whitefish caviar
Chervil leaf
3 Tbsp. / 45 mL white wine cream sauce/beurre blanc

Sauté cabbage and onion in the butter and add potato, trout and shrimp. Season. Warm poached egg and wilted spinach.

Arrange hash on one side of the plate and on other place egg on top of spinach, garnished with caviar and chervil. Circle a cordon of cream sauce around hash and egg.

Serves 1.

Baked Crab Cakes

Anne Milne, *chef/consultant, Vancouver*

One of my favorite things to do in my Vancouver Sun "Carte Blanche" column each Saturday is a round-up, a survey, a sampling of goodies. Breads; desserts; great soups; sweetbreads; potato chips; Christmas Day dinners; champagne bottle sizes; gift cookbooks; memorable dinners in Berlin, Regina, Buenos Aires and Healdsburg CA; "splodgewiches," gelati and oysters. In fact, the oyster survey last year turned up so many great favorites it became an entire section in this book.

In the spring of 1992 I went looking for crab cakes and found at least a dozen favorite ways from as many chefs. I would most certainly have asked Anne Milne for her recipe too, had she not been off in Beijing setting up that city's first full-blown Italian trattoria in a Shangri-la Hotel.

She came back and I did eventually ask her.

2 lbs. / 1 kg fresh or frozen crabmeat
½ bunch cilantro, chopped
½ bunch parsley, chopped
1 large garlic clove, minced
1 medium shallot, chopped
1 tsp. / 5 mL minced ginger
2 green onions, chopped
1 small red pepper, diced
1 large celery stalk, diced
3 eggs
¾ cup / 175 mL breadcrumbs (Anne prefers Panko's "Japanese style")
1 Tbsp. / 15 mL Dijon mustard
Juice of 1 lemon
Dash Tabasco
Dash Worcestershire sauce
Salt and fresh pepper as you like it

Breading

2 cups / 500 mL flour
2 eggs
¼ cup / 50 mL milk
2 cups breadcrumbs
¼ cup / 50 mL vegetable oil for frying

Squeeze water out of crabmeat by pressing in a colander. Combine all ingredients and mix well in a big bowl. Use an ice cream scoop to make uniform-sized cakes and arrange on cookie sheet. Bread the cakes in this order using 3 separate containers: flour, beaten eggs and milk, crumbs.

Flatten the cakes with a knife. Heat the oil in a skillet and brown cakes on both sides and replace cakes on cookie sheet. Bake in a 350°F (180°C) oven for 10 minutes.

Serves 6.

33

Accompaniment
Southern black bean stew and sweet corn salsa, or okra steamed with lemon and filé gumbo spice

Wine
Big, fat, lawn-clippings-style California sauvignon blanc

34

Salmon in White Zinfandel with Snow Peas and Lemon

Claude St. Onge, *Victoria*

Accompaniment
Red and green lettuce salad with pecans

Wine
Shenandoah White Zinfandel from California or Sumac Ridge Okanagan Blush from B.C.

The Sobons, Leon and Shirley, are proprietors of Shenandoah Vineyards in California's Amador County, which means they must be making zinfandel, right? Right. Big, round, spicy, bramble-berry dinner reds. Of course, there's also white zinfandel, or, as I heard someone say in a restaurant not all that long ago, "I didn't know zinfandel also came in red!"

White zin is the big wine success story of North America and while many put it down as being "amateur" wine or kids' stuff, most of those tend to be wine snobs with a serious income. Winemakers and people who have no hang-ups about what they like just keep on gulping.

Like many California vintners, the Sobons collect recipes and once in a while send a few out. One such reached me when I was busy writing the wine column for the Victoria Times-Colonist.

The combination of white zinfandel, crunchy snow peas, tangy lemon and fresh salmon with ginger, chives and garlic over fresh pasta is beautiful, particularly in spring and summer, or anytime you've caught a big one.

½ lb. / 250 g fettuccine
½ cup / 125 mL Shenandoah White Zinfandel
½ cup / 125 mL water
1 lb. / 500 g salmon fillet cut in ½" / 1.5 cm strips
2 Tbsp. / 25 mL fresh lemon juice
2 Tbsp. / 25 mL chopped fresh ginger
1 clove garlic, chopped
3 Tbsp. / 45 mL butter, cut in ½" / 1.5 cm pieces
½ lb. / 250 g snow peas, blanched 2 minutes in salted water, drained
Salt and pepper to taste
2 Tbsp. / 25 mL fresh chives or green part of scallion, chopped
1 tsp. / 5 mL lemon zest, grated

Cook pasta according to package directions. In a small saucepan bring wine and water to a boil. Add salmon strips, reduce heat to simmer and poach about 2 minutes. Remove salmon and reduce stock to ½ cup (125 mL).

Add lemon juice, ginger and garlic and remove pan from heat. Stir in butter until sauce thickens. Salt and pepper it to your taste, toss in pasta, snow peas, salmon. Sprinkle with chives and lemon zest.

Serves 2.

St. Patrick's Salmon

Wolfgang von Wieser, *Chartwell,*
The Four Seasons Hotel, Vancouver

*Some day in another venue I must tell
you my theory about why you can fly
all night across the Atlantic, get in a
car and drive through County Cork,
sit down to dinner with a lot of
Bordeaux, and then lounge around a
blazing fire with a bottle of Irish
whiskey for hours singing songs and
feel just fine in the morning.*

It's something in the distillation.

*After a couple of decades of having
strayed from the whiskey fold I came
back and became an Irish whiskey
fan all over again. All right, so it took
a tour of duty in Dublin's fair city to
do it.*

*When the fascinating touring
revival meeting known as the Irish
Whiskey Challenge came to Vancouver,
The Four Seasons' Wolfgang von
Wieser rose to one more challenge and
created this grand appetizer. No need
to wait for March either.*

14-oz. / 500 g piece frozen and thawed
   coho salmon (because this dish is not
   cooked)
2½ Tbsp. / 40 mL Jameson Irish
   Whiskey
4 Tbsp. / 60 mL extra virgin olive oil
2½ Tbsp. / 40 mL fresh lime juice
2 oz. / 50 g salt cod, grated
Freshly ground black pepper
Black sesame seeds
Basil, thyme, oregano, chopped
Grilled leeks or spring onions for
   garnish

Slice the salmon thinly and place on a
plate. Whisk together whiskey, olive
oil and lime juice and brush mixture
on the fish. Sprinkle salmon with
grated salt cod, black pepper, sesame
seeds and fresh herbs. It's ready to
serve when the fish turns opaque
(about half an hour). Garnish with
grilled leeks or onions.

It's a tasty first course. Be prepared
for requests for seconds.

Serves 2 to 4.

Accompaniment
Irish brown bread
and salted butter

Wine
Jameson's famed
barley wine

36

Grilled Pacific Coast Halibut

Bernard Casavant, *Wildflower Restaurant, Chateau Whistler Resort*

The Chateau Whistler's fresh-food fiend Bernard Casavant continues to make West Coast waves with his locally foraged foods. Greens, herbs, meats and fish, fruit and anything else that may lurk out there in the not-too-distant wilds is fair game for his fertile brain and brilliant kitchens.

For the CP Hotel chain's 125th birthday he called for a special bottling of Mission Hill Johannisberg Riesling and then paired it with this fish dish that's simple and so tasty.

4 halibut fillets, 5 oz / 140 g each,
   boned and skinned
4 Tbsp. / 60 mL dry sherry
2 Tbsp. / 25 mL light soy sauce
2 Tbsp. / 25 mL oyster sauce
2 Tbsp. / 25 mL fresh lemon juice
2 Tbsp. / 25 mL sesame oil
½ tsp. / 2 mL freshly ground black
   pepper
Finely minced chives
Finely minced fresh ginger root
2 Tbsp. / 25 mL cooking oil

Put halibut in a ceramic bowl. Mix all ingredients except oil and pour over fish. Marinate at least 2 hours, preferably overnight, turning fish occasionally.

Turn grill or barbecue to medium (350 to 400°F / 180 to 200°C) and lightly oil grilling surface with cooking oil. Cook fish approximately 10 to 12 minutes, turning once and basting with marinade all the while.

Serves 4.

Accompaniment
Ginger-mango salsa (just the fresh fruit, chopped, with a little minced ginger and black pepper); sundried-tomato focaccia bread

Wine
Okanagan Johannisberg riesling

FOWL

*Here's a bird for every pot;
a finger-licking of tasty
possibilities . . . stop me before
I metaphorize again!*

38

Gilroy Was Here Garlic Chicken

Garlic is good. Garlic should run the country, save the environment, wipe out cholesterol and so on. Of course, it already does some of that stuff. Everyone knows of the famous forty-cloves-of-garlic chicken. How many have had the nerve—and the supply of garlic—to actually try it!?

This is a subcompact version calling for only five cloves, though there's nothing says you can't double up. The recipe is adapted from a cook-off winner at the Gilroy Garlic Festival. Drive south from San Francisco until, maybe an hour, an hour-and-a-quarter along, you suddenly start to get unmistakable whiffs of . . . garlic. That'll be your Gilroy, garlic capital of the world, dead ahead.

Accompaniment
Mashed potatoes

Wine
Cheap champagne
or other oxymoronic
wine

5 cloves fresh garlic
1 Tbsp. / 15 mL lemon juice
4 large pieces frying chicken
2 Tbsp. / 25 mL butter
1 Tbsp. / 15 mL oil
1 cup / 250 mL mushrooms, sliced
¾ cup / 175 mL dry white wine
1 bay leaf
½ tsp. / 2 mL salt
1-2 cups / 250-500 mL chicken broth
1 tsp. / 5 mL Dijon mustard
1 Tbsp. / 15 mL parsley, chopped

Peel and mash 1 clove of the garlic and mix with lemon juice. Rub all the chicken pieces with this and let sit for 10 minutes.

Melt butter and oil, add chicken and sauté on medium for 15 minutes, turning once. Add mushrooms, wine, bay leaf, salt and the rest of the garlic as whole cloves. Cover and cook 10 minutes. Blend broth and mustard and pour over chicken. Continue cooking, covered, another 10 to 15 minutes.

Take chicken pieces and garlic cloves out of the pan and keep warm. Throw out the bay leaf and bring liquid to a boil in the pan to reduce and thicken a little. Pour over the chicken and sprinkle parsley on top.

Serve a soft-cooked garlic clove with each portion to mash into the sauce while eating the chicken.

Serves 4.

Duxoup's Dux

Duxoup Wine Works, Healdsburg, California

Transplanted Minnesotan, music major, opera fan, lover of cats and all-around-good-guy Robert Andrew Cutter operates the Duxoup Wine Works, along with his wife Deborah, in Sonoma County's Dry Creek Valley. Closest town of any consequence is Healdsburg. Nearest neighbors include a few big-league names: Ferrari-Carano, Preston, Quivira.

No tours, no tasting room, no gift shop. Good wines though, all of them red. The Cutters do it all from crush to shipping, except when sleuthsome visitors come calling and are pressed into duty pasting labels on the bottles or helping turn the one-at-a-time bottling line.

I found Duxoup quite a few years ago after a tip from my Healdsburg friend Mildred Howie, who knows everything about wine in these parts. I was intrigued by the name. Was it some obscure bit of country-French I didn't know or a tip of the hat to the Marx Brothers? Right on Number 2.

But you can still hear people ordering it in restaurants, usually in California and usually not Dry Creek locals. "We'll have a bottle of the Doo-zoo Zinfandel, s'il vous plaît," (the "p" presumably silent as in ptarmigan).

Duck-soup—that's the pronunciation, just like it's Chateau St. Jean as in the prime of Miss Brodie and not the prime minister. There's only a little Duxoup to be found in Canada and not all that much outside California, at all.

Now and then a note arrives from the wine works offering some observation—culinary, musical, oenological or just plain silly. Among the handful of recipes the Cutters have generated, this is the one I like the best. It's also one of the easiest.

1 Tbsp. / 15 mL coarse salt
2 Tbsp. / 25 mL finely minced shallots
2 Tbsp. / 25 mL chopped parsley
1 bay leaf, crumbled
Pinch thyme
4 or more garlic cloves, finely diced
2 tsp. / 10 mL paprika
1 tsp. / 5 mL cayenne
1 tsp. / 5 mL chili powder
Fresh black pepper to taste.
4 duck breasts

Mix all dry marinade ingredients in a bowl. Roll duck breasts in the mixture and place skin side down in a dish. Cover and let sit in the fridge for at least 12 hours, preferably overnight.

Wipe off excess marinade. Grill or broil for 1 to 2 minutes, 4 inches (10 cm) away from heat, with skin side down. Turn duck over, score skin side with a knife and cook another 4 minutes. Remove meat from heat and let rest a few minutes.

"Follow the next instructions to the letter!" says the memo. "Serve with Duxoup Syrah."

Serves 4.

Accompaniment
Garlic bread, roasted potatoes, French potato salad

Wine
As noted

Chicken with Beans, Peas and Okra, plus Pasta and Harissa

This is a simple way of cooking chicken with a very hot Moroccan seasoning/sauce called harissa. The lima beans and peas and green beans—plus the sliced okra—provide all the starchy vegetable stuff, and there's even pasta to carbo-load. Chicken thighs, with the skin on and the bones in, are the ticket; for some reason I don't think the skinned, boneless ones taste as good, plus they cost a lot more. I've made it once or twice with cubes of good lamb, which is a nice change of taste. The okra is optional; not everyone likes the taste and texture. But don't try to make it without harissa, which gives it its distinctive fiery North African tang.

Harissa
(wear rubber gloves while processing)
- 4 dried red chili peppers
- 2 cloves garlic, peeled and chopped
- 1 Tbsp. / 15 mL caraway seeds
- 1 tsp. / 5 mL ground cumin
- 1 tsp. / 5 mL ground coriander seed
- 1 tsp / 5 mL (or more) kosher salt
- Olive oil

Soak chilies in warm water for 1 hour. Drain, cut into small bits and pound in a mortar (I like it *really* hot, so I leave the seeds in). Add garlic, all spices and salt. Pound into a paste, spoon into a small jar and pack tightly with spoon. Pour on good-quality olive oil to cover and seal the condiment.

Keeps almost indefinitely in the fridge, diminishing its fire after a while. Remove the "topping" of oil before using if you like, though it softens the intensity a little. Always replace the protective layer of oil.

Harissa also goes nicely with green and black olives tossed in it, as finger food. Watch where you put the fingers, though.

Chicken

- 12 chicken thighs
  (or corresponding amount of lamb)
- ½ cup / 125 mL olive oil
  (not extra virgin)
- Cayenne, salt and pepper to taste
- 3 large onions, coarsely chopped
- 5-6 large celery sticks and leaves,
  coarsely chopped
- 1 cup / 250 mL green beans (fresh if it's
  that time of the year, otherwise
  frozen work well; defrost and drain;
  avoid canned!)
- 1 cup / 250 mL baby lima beans
- 1 cup / 250 mL shelled green peas
- 1 tsp. / 5 mL kosher salt
- 10 medium ripe tomatoes (2 large tins
  Italian plum tomatoes, drained)
- 1 pkg. frozen okra, drained and
  chopped
  (or 1 can Bruce's pieces, drained)
- 6-8 tsp. / 30-40 mL fresh lemon juice
- 1 lb. / 500 g medium-sized pasta
  (penne, farfalle, etc.), cooked al
  dente
- ½ cup / 125 mL fresh coriander
  (cilantro), chopped
  (or ½ / 125 mL cup parsley)
- ½ / 125 mL cup hazelnuts, roasted
- 2 Tbsp. / 25 mL harissa (if you dare,
  but experiment with your achieved
  level of fire before inflicting on
  unsuspecting guests)

Brown chicken thighs well in oil in a big pot, sprinkling with cayenne, salt and pepper. Take chicken out, keeping the oil and bits in the pot, and brown the onions and celery. Put chicken back in and add beans and peas and the kosher salt. Add tomatoes, okra and lemon juice. Cover and bake in a 325°F (160°C) oven for 35 to 45 minutes, checking chicken and veggies periodically for tenderness.

Stir in the cooked pasta, chopped coriander, hazelnuts and harissa. Taste for seasoning—you may want to add more salt, pepper, lemon juice, even harissa, if it's too tame. Let the pot come to a final simmer once more, on top of the stove if you like, and serve.

Serves 6, anyway.

Accompaniment
Good and cold green salad, mealy bread

Wine
Much cold beer or cider; margaritas; Tunisian fig eau de vie and Coke

Game Hens in Green Sauce

I was nicely surprised to find Cornish game hens in the fresh case at the supermarket not long ago. I remembered all the stories (which are probably apocryphal) about Victor Borge and how they were bred to specifications for the CPR. I've never been able to substantiate them. Fine—even if he'd done nothing other than his "Inflationary Alphabet" skit, he'd be assured a spot in heaven.

I was not so nicely surprised when I went to the checkout and found that the little birdies were $11.95 apiece. Seems last time I bought them they were 99 cents each.

The sauce for this is a variation on the South American salsa verde. The seeds/nuts, the leaves/lettuces, even some of the spices are variable according to what you can find and what you like to taste. Garlic, parsley, hot peppers and cilantro are pretty well essential though, and tomatillos are wonderful in this. No, green tomatoes aren't a real substitute—they taste different—but go ahead. On the other hand, if you've always wondered what those little green things with the husks were and how to use them, here's a trial run.

The sauce is excellent for cooking chicken in or even firm fish like a good slab of halibut; sausages too—chorizo, Nürnberger bratwurst, debreciner, whatever—we cross all boundaries with ease.

Birds
  Chicken or game hens cut in pieces, enough for 4 people
  6 garlic cloves
  1 bay leaf
  1 large onion, chopped

Put poultry pieces in big pot, cover with cold water, add garlic, bay leaf, onion and salt. Heat to boiling, turn down and simmer 20 minutes. Strain liquid and reserve. Bring pot to simmer over moderate heat and cook for 25 to 35 minutes.

Remove chicken to warmed platter.

Green Sauce

¼ cup / 50 mL black sesame seeds

¼ cup / 50 mL white sesame seeds
(double up on the white if there's no
Thai market near you)

¼ cup / 125 mL shelled pepitas
(raw pumpkin seeds)

3 large garlic cloves, halved

3 large green onions, chopped

¾ lb. / 350 g tomatillos, husked,
rinsed in warm water and quartered

3 cups / 750 mL chopped escarole and
romaine leaves

3-4 jalapeños, seeded and chopped

1 cup / 250 mL parsley, chopped

1 cup / 250 mL cilantro, chopped

1½ cups / 375 mL chicken broth (from
game hen cook pot or canned), hot

6-8 Tbsp. / 90-120 mL fresh lime juice

2 Tbsp. / 25 mL sugar

Ground black pepper to taste

Toast sesame seeds and pepitas in an iron frying pan. Cool. Grind the seeds in a spice mill (or coffee grinder you don't use for anything else) or pound with pestle, in mortar. Put garlic, green onion, tomatillo, escarole and romaine, jalapeños, parsley, cilantro and ground seeds in the blender or food processor and purée. Add hot chicken broth and process 'til nice and smooth.

Just before serving, stir lime juice and sugar into the green sauce, add salt and pepper to taste, and spoon the sauce over the chicken.

Serves 4.

Accompaniment:
Nice dry rice; black beans (buy canned and heat 'em with a little extra onion and pepper or make Armando Diaz's beans from elsewhere in this collection); hot tortillas

Wine
Margaritas; maybe iced vinho verde

Steamed Chicken with Sweet-Savory Pasta Stuffing

If you find those aforementioned game hens (see the preceding recipe) and your budget can stand it, get a couple more and try this one next. The chicken is steamed in what becomes a fragrant stock and the stuffing is surprising with all those Christmas spices.

I love the way the North Africans cook chicken, with honey and sweet spices, nuts and raisins, in paper-thin pastry as in a b'stilla and in recipes like this one. It takes longer than you might think to steam even a small chicken. Pasta should be tiny; orzo is almost too big—my old standby stelline certainly so. There are "pepper-corns" (acini de pepe) or "melon seeds" (semenza di melone) which are about right.

The stuffing is seriously yummy and it's not a bad idea to make a little extra and put it in a cheesecloth bag and cook it with the chicken.

2 cups / 500 mL tiny pasta, cooked
    extra al dente
3 Tbsp. / 45 mL chopped walnuts
    (or half pecans)
3 Tbsp. / 45 mL chopped toasted
    almonds
3 Tbsp. / 45 mL white raisins, chopped
2-3 Tbsp. / 25-45 mL butter, melted
1/4 tsp. / 1 mL ground cumin
1/4 tsp. / 1 mL ground cinnamon
1/8 tsp. / 0.5 mL ground ginger
1/8 tsp. / 0.5 mL ground allspice
1/4 - 1/2 tsp. / 1-2 mL ground white
    pepper
2 Tbsp. / 25 mL honey
1 chicken or 2 game hens
    (to 4 1/2 lbs. / 3 kg)
Salt to taste
Butter and olive oil for browning

Combine the drained cooked pasta with the nuts, raisins, melted butter, spices and honey. Blend thoroughly. Stuff the chicken with the mixture. Close cavities with string or skewers (string's easier to accommodate the browning at the end). Truss chicken well to keep stuffing from escaping.

Prepare a steamer with boiling water and place rack about 1 to 1 1/2 inches (2.5 to 4 cm) over water. Put chicken on the rack breast-up and boil water again. Cover steamer and cook over medium for 1 hour, check-ing after 40 minutes for doneness (you want chicken tender and not pink). When cooked, remove from steamer, let cool a little and pat dry carefully. Sprinkle salt on the chicken.

In a big pan heat butter and oil. Quickly brown the chicken on all sides. Carve and spoon out stuffing.

For 4 or more, depending on the size of the bird.

Accompaniment
The stuffing is your pasta course and any vegetables you may want to serve should be quite bland to go with the sweetness of the dish. Fresh figs are nice chilled, as a "salad." Chestnut soufflé afterwards; a little dolce latte gor-gonzola with white celery stalks and plain Tuscan bread...

Wine
A light red or a fragrant, fairly big Italian white

MEAT

*You can skip this section
if you don't do meat
and still won't go hungry.*

46

Murchie's Best Lamb Roast

This is another of those recipes that have been in the favorites file for so long I can't recall much of their origins. It's a breakfast roast, so to speak. Murchie's Best beans are what wake us up most mornings as the ancient, steam-generated grinder wheezes into action, startling the cat and grinding those little babies into coffee. It's been the roast of choice around the house for more years than I'm prepared to admit in public. Somewhere along the line came the suggestion to combine a cuppa coffee with a little leg of lamb and the rest is . . . here.

I cooked this dish for some Vancouver chefs to launch a book years back. It worked then and it's worked every time. For sandwiches the next day, discard the vegetables, reheat the sauce with some slices of lamb in it and put it on your toast! A cherry Danish on the side and there's complete nutrition. Whatever you do, don't use Sweet 'N Low or non-dairy creamer.

4-5 lb. / 1.75-2.25 kg leg of lamb, ready for roasting
Softened butter to rub on the lamb
Salt and pepper as you like it
2 cups / 500 mL chopped onions
2 cups / 500 mL chopped carrots
2 cups / 500 mL chopped celery
1 cup / 250 mL broth (lamb, if you have any; chicken's fine; beef, in a pinch)
2 cups / 500 mL Murchie's Best Roast coffee, double-strength
¾ cup / 175 mL whipping cream *
1-2 Tbsp. / 15-25 mL sugar
Fresh dill, parsley and chives, chopped fine for garnish

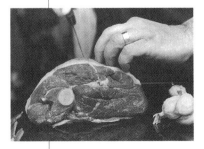

Preheat oven to 425°F (220°C). Rub lamb all over with butter and sprinkle on salt and pepper to taste. Put lamb fat side down in a roasting pan big enough to accommodate all the vegetables to come. Toss chopped onions all around and put pan in oven for 30 minutes.

After half an hour, turn the roast fat side up, cook another 15 minutes, remove the lamb from the pan and skim off as much fat as you can (don't lose the onions, though). Put lamb back in the pan and toss the carrots and celery over and around. Drop oven temperature to 350°F or 375°F (180°C or 190°C) depending on how efficient your oven is, and roast 20 minutes more. Pour in the broth and roast for another 15 minutes.

Make the coffee super strong, double or better, in your usual way. Stir in the cream (*none of that half-and-half—this is serious cholesterol we want, for flavor) and sugar 'til it's all blended and dissolved.

Back to the lamb. Add the coffee to the lamb pan and continue roasting for another 30 to 40 minutes, basting often. Check for doneness, take lamb out and carve on a hot platter.

Strain pan juices into saucepan, discarding any of the veggie bits, and stir in the fresh dill, parsley and chives (or sprinkle on dried). Pour sauce over the sliced lamb and serve.

Serves 6 with enough left over for sandwiches.

Accompaniment
Tiny roast potatoes or buttered noodles or fluffy rice. (The cooked vegetables get a lovely caramelized taste. They don't look too hot but they taste pretty good. I usually put them in a little bowl and offer them to those who want.)

Wine
Cappuccino? But seriously folks—pinot noir from France, California, Oregon is my favorite with lamb. Blue Mountain Pinot Noir from the Okanagan is a rare and splendid treat.

48

Chopped Lamb with a Trinity of Garlic

Dagobert Niemann, *Vancouver*

Dagobert Niemann had a wonderful place in Gastown known as La Brochette. Here he had a tournebroche, roughly the size of the Eiffel tower, and on a rainy, misty night you splodged through the Gastown puddles to get here (there was never any parking nearby) and sat yourself in the front of the restaurant within hailing distance of the tournebroche and watched him make things on and with it: pieces of beef, birds, kidney, whatever.

It was wonderful food, wonderfully cooked, and finally after one too many arguments with the landlord, Niemann hired the population of a small European country to take the tournebroche out and move it to his home in the Fraser Valley. Rumor has it they took out a couple of overpasses around Abbotsford in the process.

Late in the spring of '95 as I'm putting these notes together, there he is sniffing around restaurant spaces, looking for some place big enough to reinstall the giant rotisserie. I offered him the cabanas by the pool but he decided the space was still too small. We may get him and his hardware—and his marvellous methods for cooking meats—on to Vancouver's North Shore yet. Stay tuned for further developments.

This recipe calls for three solid hits of garlic. If this bothers you, psychologically or physiologically, cosmetically or spiritually, read no further. Otherwise, dive in and make sure those in your immediate personal space dive in with you. I'd even invite my dentist if there's any sort of check-up appointment in next month's DayTimer.

Not so much a recipe as a martial arts course, this . . . It consists of any good cut of lamb (though a leg is probably best), lamb jus and a good aioli.

Notes and observations in quotes are Dag Niemann's own.

Jus

Leg of lamb (ask the butcher for bones if you buy boneless meat)
1 large onion, chopped
1 large carrot, chopped
½-1 celery stalk
1 cup / 250 mL wine
½ cup / 125 mL stock
Flour (optional)

Bone the lamb and refrigerate meat. Roast the bones in a hot oven with vegetables scattered around. Deglaze the pan with wine and broth, then put all the contents into a pot and cook for about an hour. Pour the mixture through a sieve, discard the solids and return the liquid to the pot, cooking 'til it has reduced to less than half. Add lots of crushed garlic at the end—not to cook with the liquid but just to heat through and flavor it.

"The jus has to be good and rich."

Accompaniment
Only bread—and lots of it—for dipping and sopping up the sauces

Wine
Sturdy pinot noir (Lange Vineyards from Oregon; Acacia's lund Vineyards from Carneros; August Kesseler's from Germany)

Aioli

France's great country garlic sauce/spread can be done various ways. Here's one I like quite a bit and another, simpler one that is tasty too.

6 large cloves garlic
½ tsp. / 2 mL salt
2-3 large egg yolks at room temperature
1 cup / 250 mL extra virgin olive oil

Peel and halve garlic (take out any green sprouts in the middle).
Put halves in a mortar or use the flat of a knife to mash, add salt and pound to a paste. Put in a larger bowl and add 1 egg yolk at a time. Using the pestle, mush the yolk around in the paste, mixing well.

After eggs are incorporated, add oil drop by drop and continue mushing until the mix starts to thicken. Now pour in oil in a very slow, steady stream, mushing all the while until you have mayonnaise consistency.

Or:

¾ cup / 175 mL really fresh eggy mayonnaise
1 large garlic clove, chopped
1½ Tbsp. / 25 mL fresh lemon juice
1 Tbsp. / 15 mL port
½ Tbsp. / 8 mL sherry vinegar
    (or 1½ Tbsp. / 25 mL amarone *plus* ½ tsp. / 2 mL balsamic vinegar)
¼ cup oil
½ tsp. / 2 mL salt
Hot pepper sauce (optional)

Whisk mayo, garlic, lemon juice, wine and vinegar together. Slowly drizzle in oil, stirring constantly. When it's reached the consistency you like, add salt and blend; add hot sauce if desired.

Lamb
Meat from the leg of lamb
A little mustard
Garlic ("Never slice it, hash it.")
Freshly ground black pepper
A little Worcestershire
A little Tabasco
A little lemon juice
A little plain yogurt
Onions, chopped
Medium-sized breadcrumbs
A little paprika
A little rosemary
A little oregano
A little thyme
A little basil
A little oil

Chop meat by hand for ultimate consistency control. You do not want it too fine. Try not to use ground lamb. Add the mustard, garlic, pepper, Worcestershire, Tabasco, lemon juice and yogurt and mix thoroughly. (The yogurt is to create cooking liquid, and it's also a nice natural "preservative" for the meat; you can use egg, which is heavier, but Niemann prefers yogurt.)

Sauté the onions, breadcrumbs and herbs and spices together in the oil for not more than 4 minutes—gently, gently. Add the mixture to the bowl

50

with the lamb. Mix well and check for seasoning. If too liquid, add some more bread crumbs.

"The lamb should be smelling wonderful by now!"

It's best to mix with the hands, continually kneading it, folding over from the sides, like bread dough. It's important to mix it very well so it won't fall apart when heated. When there are no more valleys, shape it into big 10-ounce (300 g) patties, or bigger 20-ouncers (550 g)! They should be nice and big and thick.

Pour some olive oil on a plate. Dip lamb patties in oil, then more bread-crumbs on each side to make a wonderful crust. "Hit it with your palms for a nice flat, even surface."

Sear in a very hot heavy skillet for 5 minutes per side to brown the meat. Pour lamb jus on a heated plate and then lamb patty, slathering on as much aioli as you can stand.

Serves a civilized number.

Lamb Chops with Chorizo and Garlic

If I were to sit and think about it for any length of time I'd have to say lamb is my favorite meat these days. It is heartier and more versatile than any other I can think of. Each cut of lamb is distinctive from any other, and if you haven't yet got 'round to the garlic-chopped lamb delight of Dagobert Niemann, go back to the previous recipe.

2 good-sized lamb chops, fat well
   trimmed
Splash of olive oil
3 large garlic cloves, peeled and halved
   or thirded
½ chorizo sausage, cut into ½"
   (1.5 cm) slices or cubes
Sprinkle of dried mint or a few fresh
   leaves, chopped
Coarse black pepper to taste
Fresh rosemary or a few dried needles
Additional herbs of your fancy or
   window-box availability
1 tootle good balsamic vinegar

Heat an unoiled iron frying pan until good and hot. Sear chops 1 minute per side. Remove from pan and pour off fat. Add a splash of olive oil and turn heat down to medium. Add garlic and chorizo and cook a couple of minutes. Return lamb chops to the pan and cook for no more than 8 minutes in total, turning now and then. (If you don't like your garlic all nutty-crunchy, you might want to take it out of the pan while the lamb cooks.)

When the smoke alarm goes off, put a lid on the pan and open all the windows. It's almost done. Two or 3 minutes before the chops have finished cooking, sprinkle with mint, pepper, rosemary and/or anything else you like. A few seconds before serving, splash in the balsamic vinegar and stir everything up.

Serve that up with a little mound of rock salt and some chopped fresh parsley on the side. Never mind all that business about flat-leaf; good ol' garden-variety curly-leaf is just fine!

Serves 2.

Accompaniment

New potatoes if there are any, boiled, with a few mixed-color peppercorns in the water. Perhaps a salad of barely steamed broccoli, slivered almonds, and a light lemony dressing.

Wine

Light red works best: valpolicella; beaujolais, pinot noir, etc.

Beef Roulades Stuffed with Enoki Mushrooms

Kam Shing Lam,
Grand King Seafood Restaurant, Vancouver

Five years ago, Chef Kam Shing Lam arrived from Hong Kong to supervise the quite-amazing kitchens of the then Dynasty restaurant, an upscale Chinese eating establishment in an even upper-scale downtown hotel. Here's where I first encountered Chef Lam's brilliant all-over-the-map cuisine.

Now, rouladen are a staple in a young German lad's diet. We had them for Sunday dinners a dozen times a year: thin slices of beef rolled around bacon, onion and dill pickle, braised in a rich sauce.

But enoki?

It's the sort of thing Lam loves to do: mix it up but always end with a taste you want to take home and curl up with. His is elaborate, high-end Hong Kong cuisine based on ancient cooking traditions but calling in a lot of creative chips from other culinary centers. Consequently, there is more than a little French in some of the sauces, a touch of California here and there, a little Japanese, some Thai-style spicing, whatever takes his fancy—even a bit of German meat-roll!

His menu items are a lovely read. I remember veal chops with gin, ribs simmered in 7-Up and something else—ever notice how really elusive the taste-memory can be?—roasted crispy-skin pigeon, sautéed scallops with deep-fried milk (!) chicken with pine nuts and olive seeds, steamed bundles of abalone, barbecued duck and sea-moss, roasted eel with a hint of honey.

This is one of his signature dishes. When I first tasted it he also used a little conpoy in the mix. It's dried scallop and many cooks just let it go at that. However, true conpoy is a particular type of scallop; my colleague from Hong Kong, William Mark, says in his recent The Chinese Gourmet: *". . . hard amber disks of a type of rare scallop . . . one of the most expensive ingredients [it] makes an appearance usually only in very special banquet meals . . . the Chinese revere it for its supreme flavour . . ." While Chef Lam hasn't called for it here, you can go right ahead and sprinkle it on; no one's looking.*

2 oz. / 55 g enoki mushrooms

½ lb. / 250 g sirloin steak

Cornstarch

½ cup / 125 mL vegetable oil

½ tsp. / 2 mL garlic, minced

2 Tbsp. / 25 mL onion, finely diced

1 lb. / 500 g broccoli spears, poached in
   salted boiling water

Chili sauce

1 tsp. / 5 mL tomato paste

1½ tsp. / 7 mL oyster sauce

Season enoki mushrooms with salt. Freeze sirloin steak and slice thinly with meat slicer. It should yield 8 slices. Allow to thaw. Lightly pat both sides of sirloin with cornstarch.

Divide enoki into 8 portions. Spread meat slices on a flat surface, place mushrooms in center and roll up the meat. Lightly pat each roulade with cornstarch and squeeze each one gently at the join.

Heat wok with vegetable oil. Brown roulades in wok for 2 minutes, remove. Drain wok of excess oil, then add garlic, onion, chili sauce, tomato paste and oyster sauce. Return roulades to wok and stir continuously for 1 minute. Remove roulades and arrange on bed of broccoli spears.

Serves 4.

53

Accompaniment
Hot rice or noodles

Wine
Côtes du Rhône or shiraz

Italian Pot Roast

Patricia Maynard Sloan, *Victoria*

Another one with a generic title hiding a wealth of wonderful flavors; hiding being an operative term here—the herbs-and-garlic "pockets" burst on the tongue when you find them. Just don't let someone scoop them all before it gets to be your turn at the roast.

This is one of the top three or four culinary memories of the famous Willis Point and one of its famous firefighters, who points out that virtually all of the ingredients can be adjusted to taste.

1 Tbsp. / 15 mL very finely chopped
   garlic
1 Tbsp. / 15 mL dried oregano
1 tsp. / 5 mL salt
2 tsp. / 10 mL freshly ground black
   pepper
10 pieces back bacon
3 lb. (1.5 kg) beef roast suitable for
   braising, all fat removed, securely tied
3 Tbsp. / 45 mL butter
1 Tbsp. / 15 mL olive oil
1 cup / 250 mL coarsely chopped onions
½ cup / 125 mL coarsely chopped
   carrots
½ cup / 125 mL coarsely chopped
   celery
1 bottle dry red wine ("a rough Chilean
   with lots of body is good")
1-2 cups / 250-500 mL coarsely chopped
   tinned tomatoes
3 bay leaves
Sufficient beef stock or canned
   consommé

Accompaniment
Start with Asparagus-prosciutto rolls (see next page); then serve roast with crusty bread and green salad, or boiled potatoes, dense pasta, something to catch all the sauce; vegetables if you've got guilt, just more meat if you haven't.

Wine
Some of that full-bodied Chilean . . .

Preheat oven to 350°F (180°C). Mix garlic, oregano, salt and pepper together and roll pieces of bacon in the mixture. With a small sharp knife cut some deep incisions in the roast and stuff the bacon into the holes. Brown beef in a cast-iron pan with 1 Tbsp. (15 mL) of the butter and the 1 Tbsp. (15 mL) oil.

In a heavy casserole melt the remaining 2 Tbsp. (30 mL) of butter. Combine onion, carrot and celery chunks on a cutting board and chop together into very small pieces. Stir mixture into the butter and cook at least 10 minutes, stirring often, until vegetables are soft and lightly browned. Put browned beef roast on top of the vegetables.

Pour any fat out of the cast-iron pan and pour in half the wine and boil over high heat, stirring constantly. When wine has reduced to about a cup (250 mL) or less, add this to the casserole along with the balance of the wine ("Minus, of course, what the cook has had"), plus chopped tomatoes, bay leaves and enough beef stock to bring liquid about halfway up the sides of the beef.

Bring to a boil over high heat on top of the stove; then cover tightly and braise in the oven for about 2 hours. Remove meat, strain the sauce and thicken with a bit of butter mixed with flour. Taste for seasoning.

Serves a bunch.

Prosciutto, Asparagus and Cream Cheese Rolls

A bunch of 3″ (7.5 cm) asparagus tips
1 Tbsp. / 15 mL spreadable cream
cheese per slice of prosciutto
Several pieces of prosciutto
Black pepper and garlic salt to taste

Blanch asparagus tips and plunge immediately into ice water.

Spread 1 Tbsp. (15 mL) of cream cheese on each piece of prosciutto. Sprinkle with freshly ground black pepper and garlic salt. Roll up asparagus in the prosciutto and refrigerate for about 2 hours. Bake in 400°F (200°C) oven until cheese bubbles.

Serves the same bunch.

56

Tanqueray'd Tenderloin

When I was busy taping twenty-six episodes of The Cooking Game, *North America's first television cooking competition, I was struck by the fact that of fifty-two different recipes that were prepared on camera, only one called for beef. Pork, fish, veal, lamb, chicken, vegetables all figured prominently but only one dish of beef. Mind you, it was the finalist's final item and it won her the Grand Prize . . . !*

It's true for me too. I cook lots of other meats these days. But I'm not about to give it up—beef, I mean— and when I feel like a hit I really need it cooked well. This dish satisfies the craving and does so for good company too. It's fast and foolproof. I generally call it beef 'n' gin which sounds a bit stark. Since Tanqueray continues to be my gin of choice, I've named it after John Tanqueray, with whom I spent many a marvellous lunch on Goswell Road in London over the years.

6 garlic cloves, halved
3 lbs. / 1.5 kg beef tenderloin, sliced
    into 1½" / 4 cm ovals
1 cup / 250 mL Tanqueray gin
3 doz. juniper berries
2 tsp. / 10 mL fresh thyme
3 Tbsp. / 45 mL butter
1 cup / 250 mL Jersey double cream or
    mascarpone cheese
Salt and fresh black pepper to taste

Accompaniment

Plain potatoes or small fresh pasta; something green and crisp

Wine

Tanqueray martinis (1 measure gin, the word "vermouth" whispered over the rim of the glass; an olive); or a good Italian red

Rub garlic all over the slices of beef. Then put the same halves of garlic in a pan with a smidge of heated butter for a couple of minutes, until the garlic just starts to get fragrant. Turf the garlic and set the pan aside.

Put the beef slices in a single layer in a big flat dish. Pour ½ cup (125 mL) of Tanqueray over the meat. Crush 2 dozen juniper berries and sprinkle all over the meat. Strip thyme from the branches and sprinkle on the meat as well. Cover the dish and refrigerate for 2 to 3 hours, turning two or three times.

Pat the meat dry and wipe off bits of thyme or juniper. Place the heavy pre-garlicked pan over high heat. When the pan is very hot add the butter and let it foam up. Arrange as many slices of meat as will comfortably fit in the pan and cook about 1½ to 2 minutes per side, until browned. Put on a warm platter and repeat with the rest of the meat, adding more butter if needed. Put slices on same platter.

Turn heat down to medium-low and add the rest of the juniper berries and gin. Cook 1 minute. Stir in Jersey cream (or mascarpone) and cook 'til blended, 2 to 3 minutes, stirring all the while. Add salt and pepper to taste. Return all the meat to the pan and cover with sauce. Heat through 1 to 2 minutes.

Serve with sauce spooned on top. Keep sauce warm for seconds.

Serves 6.

Veal Farmers' Style (Vitello alla contadina)

Robert Le Crom, *Hotel Vancouver*

One from the country by way of the Hotel Vancouver's kitchens and their current complement of French chefs (at least, at the time of this writing), notably, Executive Chef Robert Le Crom.

It seems so simple, doesn't it? Well, it is, apart from the slicing and filling and tying and rolling. Just make sure the knife is very sharp, the oil and butter very hot, the herbs fresh, and the almonds too. Don't use the little bag you've had in the pantry for eleven years. Go out and buy some fresh, just for this.

2 lbs. / 1 kg boneless leg of veal, membrane removed
½ lb. / 250 g pancetta
Salt and pepper to taste
6 leaves sage
½ cup / 125 mL finely ground almonds
½ cup / 125 mL butter
¼ cup / 50 mL oil
2 sprigs rosemary
1 cup / 250 mL white wine
½ cup / 125 mL chicken or veal stock

Cut veal leg lengthwise into 3 pieces. Spread pancetta slices on each piece and season with a little salt and pepper, to taste. Spread sage leaves on each piece. Tie the veal pieces together, rolled or layered, with kitchen twine. Roll in ground almonds.

In a roasting pan melt the butter with the oil. Over a burner, sear the meat. Add rosemary, white wine and stock. Cover pan and finish cooking in 400°F (200°C) oven. It should take about 45 minutes, depending on the thickness of the leg.

Serve sliced with its own sauce. This dish is not particularly eye-appealing but it will taste divine.

Serves 2 hearty eaters, 4 who don't know each other very well.

Accompaniment
Something to soak up that sauce: polenta, orzo or another small pasta, arborio rice (you can cook it just like pasta)

Wine
Substantial sauvignon blanc or one of the new Okanagan varieties: kerner, ortega, auxerrois—something white with a little natural sweetness to it; or a light red, even a blush

Sizzling, Savory (Solitary) Saltimbocca

Gianni Picchi,
Il Giardino di Umberto, **Vancouver**

It was a dark and stormy night. That was only the first mistake. Second, the fact it was a Friday. Plus it was ten P.M. *The sounds my stomach made would have muffled Metallica.*

I'd been to a restaurant opening that night. Twice a year, maybe, I go to an official restaurant opening, if only to remind myself why I don't go to restaurant openings. Mostly because there's never any food.

This one ran to form: a lot of serious liquid—martinis, wine in all official colors—plus people milling about, all edgier than cats in a roomful of rocking chairs, trying to suss out some sustenance.

Now and again a platter of something appeared, only to be hoovered by the hungry. Upstairs, nursing another martini, I was next to the bar but next to nothing foodwise.

It took me an hour to get to the front door, cutting off people in mid-well-wish, unhooking the hangers-on, mixing briefly with the multiple media, slivering through the slipstream of folks who looked like they weren't getting out much.

Once out, I was in it: the aforementioned dark and stormy. Ten-to-ten blinked the dashboard LCD. This town shuts down tight most nights. Fridays, maybe ten-thirty, quarter to eleven if it's balmy.

I had visions of Lenny's or McDougall's or Burger Pig or Substrate: one of those drive-by eateries where people have nanosecond smiles. By this time it was way too late for me to want to have a nice day.

Close-ups of dinner dishes clicked through my head like a bad slide show at a chef's house: pasta with pesto and parmesan—click. Kidneys in mustard sauce with rice—click. Saltimbocca—click. Omelets with chives and sour cream and caviar—click. Saltimbocca. Again? Hold that frame.

I'd practically forgotten how good it was until, somehow, the wall with the blistering green letters, the proximity of the yellow house, the unusually dense concentration of stockbrokers on the sidewalk out front, made me realize my mind had miraculously magnetized me to the corner of Hornby and Pacific. Right again—Il Giardino.

It was Friday night. Room at the inn? I doubted it. But the valet parking here can work in your favor. I pull up, get out in leisurely fashion, leave the lights on and the car running, make like I've had a reservation for decades. Someone takes the car away and there it is, you're better than halfway.

Inside, the usual scene: a crush of people scoffing pasta. The place humming, the bar busy, the lights warm and cozy. The kitchen frantic, the servers frantic-squared.

Any number of impossibly thin women in black at the desk with the books where my name isn't. Little guys smoking cigars at each other in the smoking section. More than one cell phone. Somebody from some movie doing some movie stuff with somebody else from some other movie.

Could you, do you think, I ask, find me a little table? I'll sit on the stairs . . . They could and they did. It took a couple of minutes and suddenly I sat, and not on the stairs either. Good smells wafted in from the kitchen.

And Gianni Picchi cooked me saltimbocca as comfort food. That's what this dish is and he cooks it sublimely.

A lot of people go to Il Giardino for a lot of different reasons. After all of those have been exhausted—takes about nine minutes of isn't-that-Al-Jolson-behind-those-Foster-Grants nudging—there remains my best reason for going: good eats. Good working staff too, who keep the table replenished with edibles and the glasses full of wine.

It was still dark by the time my car found me again but the storm had blown over. There are a million restaurant stories in this city. This was only one of them.

A 1-serving hunk of the best veal money can buy (¼″ thick—less than 1 cm)
Some beautiful, well-aged prosciutto
Leaves of fresh unblemished sage
A little flour
A little butter
A drop of olive oil
Sufficient white wine
1 lemon, halved
Sufficient very light veal (or chicken) stock

Sandwich sage leaves between veal and prosciutto, fixing the prosciutto with toothpick if necessary. Dust with flour. Have a hot saucepan handy with a little butter and drop of oil in it, nice and hot. Put saltimbocca in, prosciutto side down, for 1 minute. Other side: 1 minute.

Pour some wine in the pan while it's still good and hot and let a little evaporate. Take veal out and set aside on hot plate. Squeeze a little lemon juice in the pan, add a bit of stock and let it all bubble up. When it moves to the middle (no more runny liquid), pour over veal and serve with half a lemon on the side.

Set some simple vegetables alongside—the simpler, the better. Cooking saltimbocca is easy but critical. Undercooked is a problem; overcooked and you've got too much saltiness.

"If you do it right, you've done a masterpiece."

Single serving.

Accompaniment
Baby potatoes, asparagus, carrots, roma tomatoes, plain pasta

Wine
Simple, fresh Italian chardonnay; shot of grappa after

Garlic Ham Marinated in Milk (Schinken mit Knoblauch und Milch)

This is a dish I recall from growing up in Berlin. I remember it was a very simple dish to make and so far as memory serves, this is how it's done. Great ham sandwiches for days after.

Accompaniment
Sliced sweet onions; scalloped potatoes; ratatouille

Wine
Pinot gris; cannonau di Sardegna; riesling from the Mosel

1 smoked ham (not Westphalian, but the
   Black Forest kind)
4-8 cups / 1-2 L milk
Lots of garlic cloves, chopped
Salt and pepper

Put the ham into a big bowl (what size ham you buy is determined by the size of available bowls). Mix milk with lots of garlic, plenty of black pepper and coarse salt. Pour over the ham (it doesn't need to be completely covered but it should reach halfway up the sides of the ham). Cover with a lid or some wrap and put ham in the fridge for 24 to 48 hours, turning five or six times in the marinade.

When it's cooking time take the ham out of the milk and heat the oven to 350°F (180°C). Put the ham in a big roasting pan and pour some of the milk over, to about 2 or 3 inches (5 to 7.5 cm) deep. Bake the ham for about 1 hour for every 3 pounds (1.5 kg) of meat. Baste every 15 minutes with reserved milk.

Cook another 45 minutes to an hour, covered with foil if you want a moist ham, or raise the temperature to 400°F (200°C) and let it get crispy.

For a family, for a week.

Elegant Prune-stuffed Pork Roast

Mirassou Vineyards, San Jose, California

*Pork is my favorite roast, with pota-
toes spattered in fat clustered around
the cooking meat, nothing too obtru-
sive by way of vegetables, a tub of
Gelato Fresco Sicilian Blood-orange
Sorbet for dessert, and some 17th-cen-
tury lute music to lull the soul.*

*Pork and prunes are almost a cliché
together, but this is such a good taste,
and anyway, the reason clichés are
clichés is that we keep coming back for
more of the same—like this roast
recipe from the fifth-generation
Mirassou wine family.*

**4 lb. / 1.75 kg boneless loin of pork,
  rolled and tied**

20 pitted prunes

Salt and pepper

1 cup / 250 mL Mirassou Pinot Noir

**2 cups / 500 mL chicken stock,
  preferably unsalted**

½ cup / 125 mL heavy cream

2 Tbsp. / 25 mL brandy

Heat oven to 325°F (160°C). Push the
handle of a wooden spoon through
the center of the pork loin from one
end to the other. Make sure it is a
sturdy spoon—I've lost more lumber
in these . . . Stuff prunes into the
cavity, filling from one end to the
other. Put meat in a roasting pan.

Brown on all sides over high heat
for 5 to 10 minutes, starting with fat
side down. Salt and pepper to taste.
Add the wine and ½ cup (125 mL) of
the chicken stock to the pan. Place in
oven fat side up and roast 45 minutes, basting occasionally. Add 1 cup
(250 mL) chicken stock and continue
roasting another 40 to 45 minutes or
until internal temperature reaches
160 to 165°F (70 to 75°C).

Place roast on a heated platter.
Remove string. Cover and keep warm
while making sauce.

Sauce

Skim excess fat from roasting pan.
Add the remaining ½ cup (125 mL)
chicken stock. Bring to a boil over
medium-high heat, scraping up
browned bits from the bottom and
sides of the pan. Add cream and
brandy. Boil until sauce is slightly
thickened. Taste, adjust seasoning,
strain. Spoon a small amount of
sauce over each serving of sliced pork
roast.

Serves 8.

Accompaniment

Plain potatoes
(roasted in the oven
with oil and rock salt
are nice too, but it
may be a matter of
overgilding this par-
ticular culinary lily);
non-mushy rice; flat
rippled noodles

Wine

The Mirassou Pinot
Noir you cooked it
with—but it's not
always readily found
in this country. The
Petite Sirah, on the
other hand, is. And
furthermore, I'd use
double the amount
of brandy in the
sauce.

Armando's Legendary Cuban Pork Roast with Black Beans and Plantains

Armando Diaz, *Vancouver*

If Armando Diaz would just get to it and open another restaurant somewhere I wouldn't have to go to the trouble of finding him and badgering him to write out these few simple instructions and there would be more room in this book for other things. But oh no—can't be bothered, can he. Well fine then, we'll do it ourselves. He still has a sensational carrot cake recipe they used to come here from New York for, so we may have to wait for the Rise of the Third Armando's after all.

Accompaniment
Fluffy white rice;
Armando's secret-
recipe Caesar salad
(I didn't have time to
get that too); carrot
cake for dessert

Wine
Couple of cold
Coronas or some
cheap Chilean merlot

Roast Pork
5 lb. / 2.25 kg pork butt roast
4 cloves garlic, crushed
Salt to taste
½ orange
½ lemon
½ tsp. / 2 mL oregano

Puncture roast with a knife in a dozen places. In a bowl mix garlic, salt, juice from the orange and the lemon, and oregano. Rub mixture all over the roast and use citrus halves to get into the knife punctures. Marinate in a bowl overnight.

Heat oven to 375°F (190°C), roast pork for 15 minutes, then lower temperature to 300°F (150°C). Cook for at least 4 hours, longer if you like it falling away.

Armando says, "If there are leftovers, it makes great sandwiches."

Black Beans

  1 lb. / 500 g dried black beans, rinsed
    and picked over

  1 large onion, chopped

  1 large green pepper, chopped

  3 bay leaves

  Salt to taste

  ½ cup / 125 mL olive oil

  1 tsp. / 5 mL oregano

  2 Tbsp. / 25 mL white vinegar

Rinse beans again and put in a pot ¾ full of water. Add half the onion and half the green pepper, and the bay leaves and salt. Bring water to a boil, then simmer gently 45 minutes to an hour or until beans are tender.

In a frying pan, heat olive oil, the rest of the onion and green pepper, and the oregano. Sauté until onions are golden brown. Mix with the black beans and add vinegar. Mash beans with a potato masher to thicken the sauce. Simmer for ½ hour over medium heat, stirring often to keep beans from sticking.

Plantains

  3 or 4 plantains

  Oil for deep frying

  Coarse salt

Peel plantains and slice into ¼ inch (5 mm) rounds. Deep-fry in hot oil until they float to the surface, like potatoes. Drain on paper towels. Double a sheet of waxed or brown kitchen paper. Put plantain slices between sheets and flatten by smashing with your hand. Deep fry again. Sprinkle lots of salt on.

Serves 4.

OYSTERS

*Coming to love them
relatively late in life,
well past thirty, I enjoy them
with missionary zeal.*

"Our Famous Oyster Soup" (Zuppa di Ostriche)

Gildo Casadei, *Bianco Nero Ristorante, Vancouver*

It sits there on the menu alongside the stracciatella and the minestrone and the soup of the giorno, *identified simply as "our famous oyster soup." The hint of anise comes from the sambuca, the little splidge of cream is a wonderful touch and don't forget to grill a big, buttery garlic crouton.*

Chef Gildo Casadei is one of the great Renaissance chefs: classically trained, able to cook anything, anytime. He's blue-sky creative and when he does "fusion" it's done with no neon, just all intrinsic flavor. His amazing pastas, many named for family members—kids, grandchildren, friends—deserve their own cookbook some day soon.

This is one of the world's great soups, pure and simple.

½ cup / 125 mL total shredded or finely diced celery, onion, carrots, garlic, parsley,
Olive oil
2-3 fresh oysters, diced
Fish bouillon or stock (if using fish bones, do not use salmon bones)
1 Tbsp. tomato coulis
1 Tbsp. / 15 mL heavy cream
½ Tbsp. / 7 mL sambuca
Cracked black peppercorns
Salt

Sauté vegetables in oil until the mix is "a little blonde" (i.e., not browned). Add diced oysters. Add hot fish stock to cover and a little more. Mix in tomato coulis, cream and sambuca. Stir in pepper and salt to taste. Heat through well and serve.

Single serving, but it multiplies easily.

Accompaniment
Grilled garlic crostini

Wine
Valdizze Pinot Frizzante; Gaja Chardonnay; Soave

66

Fresh Pacific Oyster Stew

Don McDougall, *Deacon Vale Farms, Mayne Island*

Postcards from Don McDougall arrive from time to time and frequently take the form of recipes. As founder of Mocha Cafe, Don pioneered the art of the intimate wine dinner—couldn't be anything else because his restaurant was pretty small. Great winemakers came to pour some of their best and Don would build a dinner around the selection. All the dinners were sold out, and although he's gone a-farming I've no doubt he will be back in the restaurant business, perhaps on one of the Gulf Islands.

His "five years of mega-muffins, Caesars and filo pastries" have left him a little wiser, perhaps a little more substantial, probably not a lot richer. "But," he says, "I still love to cook."

So here is one to dazzle your friends or to give to someone as a present on the condition that you are invited for dinner. But be sure to take the wine.

I can be there by 7:30 . . .

Accompaniment
Cheddar Cheese
Bread (follows)

Wine
Pinot blanc

16 medium oysters with liquor
1 cup / 250 mL dry white wine
1 cup / 250 mL water
2 slices quality smoked bacon (optional)
3 cups / 750 mL diced vegetables
   (carrots, celery, onions, potatoes)
Enough milk to make 2 cups (500 mL)
   with vegetables
1 cup / 250 mL heavy cream
Salt and fresh pepper
1 Tbsp. / 15 mL chopped fresh parsley

Poach oysters with wine, water and oyster liquor for 5 minutes. Strain and save the stock. Sauté bacon until well cooked. Add vegetables and continue to sauté until tender, being careful not to let vegetables color. If you're not using bacon, sauté vegetables in a little oil.

Add enough milk to the vegetables to make 2 cups (500 mL).

Add the poaching liquid and milk with vegetables and bring to a slow boil. Skim off any froth and simmer for 15 minutes. Add oysters and heavy cream and simmer for 5 minutes, skimming frequently. Season with salt and pepper. Add chopped parsley and serve.

Serves 4 to 6.

Don McDougall's Cheddar Cheese Bread

2 1/4 cups / 550 mL all-purpose flour
3 tsp. / 15 mL baking powder
3/4 tsp. / 4 mL baking soda
1 tsp. / 5 mL salt
3 eggs
3/8 lb. / 280 g soft butter
1 cup / 250 mL buttermilk
2 cups / 500 mL grated cheddar cheese

Preheat oven to 325°F (160°C). Mix together all dry ingredients. In a separate bowl beat eggs into softened butter. Add buttermilk and cheese. Fold dry mixture into wet quickly, being careful not to overmix. Pour into greased loaf pan. Bake for 45 minutes.

Peppered Oysters with Roasted Corn and Tomato Relish

Karen Barnaby,
The Fish House in Stanley Park, Vancouver

Karen Barnaby cooks everything with big, hearty flavors and she loves it spicy, whether it's peppered prawns at a Vintners' Brunch or veal shank in a rich dark beer sauce at the first (and so far only) Beermakers' Dinner I ever attended, or a crunchy-creamy risotto with mushrooms and major cheese, or something hearty with lentils and beans or a serious meatloaf, or a fabulous fresh fish. We're talking NO FEAR cooking.

This searing platter of oysters was first served to me at someone's house. Karen had just decided to come and do a little cooking on one of her days off. This recipe was the appetizer and while the other items on the menu were wonderful too, she could have just tripled this one and we'd have found a few more bottles of bubbly and slabs of bread . . .

After this (and the aforementioned bread and bubbly, etc.) all you need is a good old Altman movie and then maybe some Almond Roca in about an hour.

And a cat on your lap, of course.

4 cups / 1 L shucked medium oysters, conserve juice
2 bay leaves
2 Tbsp. / 25 mL black peppercorns
8 cloves garlic, roasted and mashed to a paste
½ tsp. / 1 mL ground allspice
1 Tbsp. / 15 mL lemon juice

In a large frying pan bring oyster juice and bay leaves to a boil. Add oysters and cook until their edges curl. Drain in a sieve over a bowl to catch the juice.

While oysters are draining, dry-roast peppercorns over medium heat until they start to smell fragrant. Grind to a powder in a (coffee) grinder.

Return oyster liquor and bay leaves to the frying pan. Add pepper, garlic and allspice. Bring to a boil. Cook, stirring frequently, until the mixture becomes pasty.

Return oysters to the pan and coat thoroughly with pepper paste. Stir in lemon juice.

Serve at room temperature or chilled, with the relish.

Serves 4 to 6.

Relish

- 1 ear fresh corn
- 4 dead-ripe plum tomatoes, peeled and seeded
- 2 green onions, thinly sliced
- 2 Tbsp. / 25 mL coarsely chopped cilantro leaves
- Salt and pepper

Preheat oven to 400°F (200°C). Cut kernels from ear of corn and spread out on a baking pan. Roast corn for 10 to 15 minutes, stirring occasionally, until corn picks up a few brown spots. Remove from the oven and cool. Combine corn with remaining ingredients and season with salt and pepper. Serve with the oysters.

"Irresistible!" says the chef. "My favorite way of eating oysters!"

Accompaniment

Something cool and bland: grilled polenta, bulgur, tabbouleh salad

Wine

If you can find one that stands up to the oysters, by all means drink it. Pitcher of beer for me or a can of Boddington's Draught Bitter.

Scrumpied Oysters (Angels in E-Types)

At Cobble Hill on Vancouver Island, Al Piggott makes cider—real cider from real cider-apples. None of your concentrate, none of your fizz-pop-sugary stuff. Fresh as a daisy and no preservatives. The kind of cider that makes your knees gradually disappear in a Yorkshire pub on a Saturday afternoon . . .

Merridale Cider is starting to build a following farther afield than just in B.C., though given the nature of the process, it's unlikely to end up in the parliamentary cafeteria.

Too bad. It might help those folks get through the day a bit better and be a little more lucid during Question Period . . .

I invented this recipe one afternoon because I knew some of these ingredients just wanted to get together. They did and with only minimal fine-tuning, the combo worked. The fine fine-tuning was done later that same day, with the same eaters. The knees, happily, did not disappear until the person who'd been dispatched to the fish store for a second supply of oysters returned.

Accompaniment
Bread and butter

Wine
What's wrong with that scrumpy that's left over, then? And another one besides . . .

6 or 12 fresh shucked oysters and liquor, (big West Coasters or small Easterners)
6 Tbsp. / 90 mL cold unsalted butter
4 Tbsp. / 60 mL finely chopped shallots (about 2 good-sized)
1 Scotch bonnet or jalapeño pepper, seeded and chopped very fine
6 slices Ayrshire bacon
Salt and pepper to taste
½ tub / about 90 g Jersey double cream
1½ Tbsp. / 25 mL apple cider vinegar
2 Tbsp. / 30 mL chives, chopped
½ cup / 125 mL Merridale Farm Scrumpy

Melt half the butter in a sturdy pan. Add shallots and hot pepper. Stir and cook 3 minutes over medium heat. Add a little oyster liquor and cook another 2 minutes. Add oysters and cook briefly (2 minutes, until edges start curling). Remove oysters with slotted spoon and keep warm.

Cook Ayrshire bacon in a frying pan (hot at first to sear, then medium) until semicrisp, the way the English like it at breakfast. Drain and reserve.

Add 1 Tbsp. bacon fat and the scrumpy to oyster pan with juices and shallots. Stir and boil, reducing by half. Add salt and pepper and cream and cook for 1 minute. Swirl in remaining butter and apple cider vinegar. Add oysters to heat through.

Put 1 or 2 oysters on a slice of bacon, roll up à la "Angels on Horseback" and secure with toothpicks. Pour sauce over and sprinkle chives on top. Serves 2.

Blue Corn-fried Oysters

Paul MacEwen, *Granite Café, Vancouver*

Paul McEwen opened West Van's Granite Café with a couple of colleagues in 1994, and during the first week I was there three times. There were good wines, pleasant people, excellent food—some of it faintly audacious, all of it fresh and splendidly seasoned.

There used to be a share-the-table appetizer platter which accommodated as many of you had come with a sampling of just about everything off the "starters" side of the menu and a basket of the assorted and excellent house breads. Simple. And brilliant. Then a chilled cheap chardonnay (say that five times quickly) from somewhere outside the European Economic Community and there's a dinner to remember.

These oysters, with the crunch of cornmeal on and about them, form part of such a platter. The jalapeño and cilantro make a marvellous, fiery statement.

4 cups / 1 L 35% whipping cream
2 Tbsp. / 25 mL smoked jalapeño purée
Juice of 1 lime
1¼ cups / 300 mL blue cornmeal
1¼ cups / 300 mL yellow cornmeal
18 Fanny Bay oysters, small-medium, shucked
1 small bunch cilantro, finely chopped
Salt to taste
2 cups / 500 mL corn oil

In a heavy saucepan, combine the cream with the smoked jalapeño purée and lime juice. Over medium heat, reduce by half carefully, ensuring cream doesn't boil. (You can add the stalks of cilantro while reducing the cream and then strain at the end, for added flavor.) When sauce is reduced, reserve and keep hot.

Combine blue and yellow cornmeal in a shallow pan or pie plate. Add some of the oyster juice to the cornmeal to make it a little mealy. Dredge oysters in the cornmeal and press lightly to coat oysters thoroughly .

In a sauté pan, add ¼ inch (5 mm) of corn oil. Over high heat bring oil to just under the smoking point. Fry oysters 3 or 4 at a time depending on the size of the pan and the oysters. Fry each oyster 30 seconds per side or until golden. Blot oil off the oysters with a paper towel. Reserve and keep warm.

Ladle 5 Tbsp. (75 mL) of sauce on a warm serving plate. Place 3 or 4 oysters on the sauce. Garnish with chopped cilantro.

Serves 6 to 8.

Accompaniment
"At Granite Café, we serve these with mixed greens and a walnut oil and sherry vinaigrette," says the chef. "Garnish with toasted sesame seeds and Japanese chili pepper." And don't forget lots of bread.

Wine
How about a margarita?

72

Oyster Jim's Clayoquot Sound Oysters

Elizabeth Fox
The Marina Restaurant, Victoria

Victoria's refurbished Marina Restaurant focuses on fish with dedication and plenty of passion in the kitchen and has a sensational, award-winning wine list—one of the best on the West Coast. The combination is irresistible, and the Oyster Jims here were so good they sparked a six-month-long oyster quest, which resulted in a best-of-the-west column and gave rise to this all-oyster section of the book.

(Also ask about the marinated Dungeness crab wrapped in a nori cone; the P.E.I. mussels with crumbled chorizo sausage and cilantro and tomato; the rack of lamb with a port, espresso and chocolate sauce, with rosemary bread pudding. I know that's not a fish but I can be open-minded about these things . . .)

Accompaniment
Bread galore

Wine
Not-too-dry champagne; a German sekt (Henkell); or Panther Creek or other Oregon Melon (hard to find but worth the search; at the Marina they list two)

2/3 cup / 150 mL fresh basil leaves
6 Tbsp. / 90 mL quality olive oil
1 Tbsp. / 15 mL horseradish
Juice of 1/4 lemon
2 Oyster Jim's or other large cooking oysters
Salt and pepper to taste
1 alderwood fire

Purée basil, oil, horseradish and lemon juice together. Season with salt and pepper.

Place oysters on the fire flat side up, either directly in the flame or on a grate. Cook until bubbles form around edge of shells. The oysters will be medium rare and shuck easily at this point. Place a tablespoon of the purée on each oyster and serve immediately.

Serves 1.

Crab-stuffed Oysters

Sue Adams, *The Amorous Oyster, Vancouver*

It's one of those little tucked-away gems most of the guidebooks tend to overlook. To the best of my knowledge no major movie stars have had any altercations here. Few stockbrokers sit in the window and smoke cigars (in fact, The Amorous Oyster was one of the first local restaurants to declare itself a completely smoke-free zone—Hurray! say some of us).

Fifteen years on, the place is still cozy and intimate and friendly, the food still fresh and imaginative, the wine list small and perfectly selected to go with the goodies. And they still (the name is your clue) focus squarely on our favorite mollusks.

The menu is written on two big blackboards on either side of the thirty-something seater and there is always the oyster sampler combo. That's the one for first-time visitors: no need to deprive yourself of old favorites like mornay and Rockefeller, black bean, Cajun, chili-pesto or Florentine. But sooner or later you'll come to the crab-stuffed model and Sue Adams does it so:

24 fresh Pacific golden mantle oysters shucked
3 slices bacon, chopped and fried very crisp
1½ cups / 375 mL breadcrumbs
¾ cup / 175 mL fresh crabmeat
½ cup / 125 mL finely chopped red bell pepper
½ cup / 125 mL finely chopped green onions
2 Tbsp. / 25 mL parmesan cheese, shredded
2 Tbsp. / 25 mL parsley
Salt and pepper to taste
Prepared béchamel sauce (or substitute mayonnaise)

Heat oven to 400°F (200°C). Place oysters in their shells on a baking tray. If using preshucked oysters, place in 4 individual lightly oiled gratin dishes. Lightly mix bacon, breadcrumbs, crab, pepper, onions, cheese, parsley and salt and pepper. Top each oyster with 1 tablespoon of stuffing mix. Place a dollop of béchamel or mayonnaise on top. Bake for 8 to 10 minutes (or 2½ to 3 minutes in the microwave, partially covered).

Serves 4 as a main-course lunch.

73

Accompaniment
Tossed wild greens salad, bread (of course)

Wine
Hainle Vineyards Estate Dry Traminer

74

Stir-fried Oysters with Black Beans and Chilies

Karen Barnaby for *Restaurant Starfish and Oyster Bar, Vancouver*

When Janice Lotzkar opened her Raintree Restaurant she brought to Vancouver something we all knew was around, though no one had ever defined it so well and so tastily before—West Coast cuisine. Ask her exactly what it is and she'll probably tell you she's still not sure, but she knows it when she tastes it. And so do all the diners who have trooped through her restaurants: first the Raintree, then North 49, the Harvest Moon in Victoria (one of the gutsiest moves I ever witnessed in the fiercely competitive restaurant business was outfitting this place with an all-and-only-B.C. wine list!) and more recently, a False-Creekside casual eatery with a new age attitude, called Starfish.

Karen Barnaby came up with this one. We're talking fire here: chilies, shreds of green onion and a mouth-searing sauce which means no alto-sax playing tonight.

1 cup / 250 mL small oysters, shucked
1 Tbsp. / 15 mL vegetable oil
1½ tsp. / 7 mL finely grated fresh ginger
2 cloves garlic, minced
1 Tbsp. / 15 mL fermented black beans
2 Tbsp. / 25 mL white wine

3 canned plum tomatoes, drained and diced
1 tsp. / 5 mL hot sauce
2 green onions, julienned

Drain oysters well and lay out on paper towels to drain further while other ingredients are prepared.

Heat oil over high heat in a wok or frying pan. Add ginger and stir-fry until it begins to turn brown. Add garlic and stir-fry until it begins to turn golden. Add black beans; as soon as they sizzle add white wine, tomatoes and hot sauce. Cook until wine evaporates, then add oysters, stir-frying until oysters firm up, about 2 minutes. Toss in green onion, stir once or twice, and serve immediately on a heated plate.

"If you want to double the recipe," the chef points out, "cook it in two batches in separate pans."

Serves 3 to 4 as an appetizer, or part of a Chinese-style meal.

Accompaniment
Bread rolls

Wine
Hogue Cellars Semillon from Washington

Oysters Zax

Zax, Steveston

One summer there was a near-the-sea seafood restaurant in scenic Steveston called Zax. Oysters were an avowed specialty and, as with many such eateries, a combination selection seemed the best way to go. There were a dozen different ones at least; some were familiar favorites and others were off-the-wall new models. Best of all was the one they named the restaurant after, or maybe it was the other way around.

I did get a copy of this simple recipe, but no one ever seemed to know who the chef was. Last time I looked, Zax was no more; at least as a name of a restaurant goes, it went. I hope that whatever changes it's undergone, someone decided to keep this tasty little dish. It's a fine party piece, an easy starter. The combination of garlic-and-wine-poached oysters, smoked salmon and hollandaise is sensational, to say nothing of rich. So it might do best to rip this page out of the book before giving it to your doctor as a gift.

3 (or 6) oysters
¼ cup / 50 mL dry white wine
1 clove garlic, crushed
3 (or 6) thin slices smoked salmon
Prepared hollandaise sauce

Poach oysters in white wine with crushed garlic. Remove from broth and wrap each oyster in a slice of smoked salmon. Place in a shallow baking dish and top with hollandaise. Place under broiler until lightly browned.

Serve hot.

Three serves 1, 6 serves 2.

Accompaniment
Bread

Wine
J. Lohr Riverstone Chardonnay from California

75

Blue Cornmeal-fried Oysters with Chipotle Cream Sauce

Doug Porter, *La Rúa in the Upper Village, Whistler*

This may run counter to course but I go to the world-famous-ski-resort-that's-practically-in-our backyard to eat. I tried skiing here once and it did nothing for my appetite but expand it. I find that I am less likely to get hurt when I sit down to a plate of La Rúa's oysters. There's no snow down my neck when the grilled quail with Pol Roger dressing comes to the table. The kind of chill I can really get next to is the one on the second-last bottle of Gaja Chardonnay. There. I said it and I'm glad.

When Mario Enero opened La Rúa, he instantly established a whole new standard in fine food for Whistler, one that most other places are still striving to approximate. By the time we all read this he'll likely have another place up and running, also above the snow-line—a bistro, according to initial plans.

I'd put a plate of oysters on the menu there too, if I were running the place.

Accompaniment
More bread
(consider investing
in a bakery)

Wine
High-end Italian
chardonnay
(Gaja or similar)

20 oysters (about 1½ lbs. or 750 g), shucked
Blue cornmeal
2 Tbsp. / 25 mL olive oil
2 Tbsp. / 25 mL minced onion
4 cloves garlic, minced
1 cup / 250 mL whipping cream
¼ tsp. / 1 mL chipotle (smoked hot pepper) sauce
3 Tbsp. / 45 mL chopped cilantro

Dip oysters in cornmeal to coat. In a skillet, heat oil over medium-high heat. Cook oysters 3 minutes on each side, until golden brown. Transfer oysters to serving plate.

Cook onion and garlic for 30 seconds, 'til slightly golden. Stir in cream and chipotle sauce and bring to a boil. Cook until slightly thickened. Stir in cilantro. Drizzle sauce over oysters.

Garnish the plate with Japanese red peppers, lemon zest and a fresh cilantro sprig.

Makes 4 servings.

Cider-poached Oysters with Leeks, Seaweed and Salmon Caviar

Le Gavroche Restaurant, Vancouver

For more years than most of us can remember, Le Gavroche has reigned supreme as the leading French restaurant out here in Lotusland. It's the place for a big-ticket dinner: two of you for romance; four of you for money; more of you for a memorable dinner party.

16-20 small oysters and liquor, shucked
4 tsp. / 20 mL unpasteurized cider vinegar
½ cup / 125 mL dry apple cider
1 medium white of leek, finely julienned
1 Tbsp. / 15 mL dried seaweed, rehydrated in cold water
1 medium shallot, finely chopped
¼ cup / 60 mL whipping cream
2 Tbsp. / 30 mL chilled butter, cut into small pieces
1 Tbsp. / 15 mL salmon caviar

In a large sauté pan, poach the oysters with their liquor, the cider vinegar, cider, leeks and seaweed until oysters are just firm to the touch. Reserve oysters on a warm plate.

Meanwhile add shallot to the poaching liquid and reduce by half over high heat. Add whipping cream and reduce by a third. Take pan off the heat and whisk in the cold butter until incorporated. Return the oysters to the sauce and gently heat through, being careful not to boil.

Stir in salmon caviar just before serving.

Serves 4 to 5.

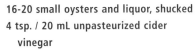

Accompaniment
French bread

Wine
Brutocao
Chardonnay from
California

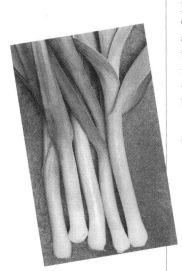

Alder-grilled Fanny Bay Oysters and Oyster Mushrooms with Jalapeño and Bacon Vinaigrette

Dan Atkinson, *Salmon House on the Hill*, *West Vancouver*

In mid-1995, Salmon House on the Hill got the critics' award from Vancouver Magazine *as best seafood restaurant, something some of us have known for a year or two. It's always nice to be vindicated by one's peers.*

Tons of alder and about equal amounts of salmon go through this fantastic room with a view every year. But Dan Atkinson also has a deft hand with spices, especially the hot ones, and Fanny Bay oysters from just across the strait.

If by any chance you ever find his Penn Cove mussels on the menu, indulge.

1 doz. Fanny Bay oysters
Oyster mushrooms
¼ cup / 50 mL chopped herbs of your
    choice—basil, thyme, parsley, dill,
    cilantro, for example
3 medium cloves garlic, peeled and
    smashed
1 cup / 250 mL malt vinegar
½ tsp. / 2 mL sea salt
1 Tbsp. / 15 mL sugar
1 Tbsp. / 15 mL whole-grain mustard
2½-3 cups / 625-750 mL olive oil
¾ cup / 175 mL alder-grilled side
    bacon, cut into lardons

3 jalapeño peppers, trimmed, cored,
    seeded, deribbed and cut brunoise
    (very, very small cubes)
1 red pepper, treated as per jalapeño
    above
1 medium red onion, washed, skinned,
    cut brunoise
1 Tbsp. / 15 mL black pepper, cracked

Grill oysters and mushrooms, preferably over alder smoke.

In blender put herbs, garlic, vinegar, salt, sugar and mustard. Blend 1 minute. Slowly add olive oil, stopping occasionally to scrape down bowl. Process until oil is fully incorporated. Pour into bowl and fold in bacon, jalapeño, red pepper, red onion and black pepper.

Serve at room temperature, with oysters, mushrooms and greens. The vinaigrette can be refrigerated for up to 2 weeks.

"Heat from the jalapeños does mellow with time," assures the chef.

Might serve 1, might serve a dozen, depending on oyster tolerances.

Accompaniment
Tuscan bread

Wine
A pinot blanc or
tokay from Alsace

Cajun Poached Oysters

Mirassou Vineyards, San Jose, California

Another one from the Mirassou family's cookbook, which I'm sure exists as an entity. This has been in my kitchen repertoire for nearly a decade. If ever there was a textbook-classic definition of the pleasures of oysters with champagne, here it is.

24 oysters, shucked, liquor reserved

6 Tbsp. / 90 mL unsalted butter

2 or more cloves garlic, minced

2 tsp. / 10 mL Cajun Magic Seafood Seasoning *

1 cup / 250 mL Mirassou Au Naturel Champagne

Reserved oyster liquor, topped up with champagne to measure 1 cup

½ cup / 125 mL parsley, chopped

1 lb. / 500 g white mushrooms, thinly sliced

Salt and pepper as required

* Paul Prudhomme's packaged spice, from the gourmet food section

79

In a small saucepan melt 2 Tbsp. (30 mL) of the butter. Add garlic and seafood seasoning and sauté for 1 minute. Add champagne and simmer 5 minutes. Add oyster liquor and 1 Tbsp. (15 mL) parsley, bring to a boil and reduce to 1 cup (250 mL).

Meanwhile, melt the remaining 4 Tbsp. (30 mL) butter in a large pan and add mushrooms. Sauté over high heat for a few minutes. Add salt and pepper and turn heat to low.

Add oysters to reduced poaching liquid and poach for 2 minutes, until edges begin to whiten and curl. Remove with slotted spoon and set aside somewhere warm. Turn heat back up to high and reduce poaching liquid some more, while dividing mushrooms onto 8 warmed plates (shallow bowls or gratin dishes are good).

Arrange 3 oysters on each plate and top with a little of the hot poaching liquid. Sprinkle with remaining parsley.

Serves 8, if they're polite.

Accompaniment
Crusty French bread

Wine
Plenty more champagne

Sloppy Gloppy Oysters

Peter Burge, *The Cannery Seafood Restaurant, Vancouver*

You can't beat the setting, especially at sunset. The Cannery looks and feels like a real cannery, sits seaside like a real cannery, and even has real photo-opportunity harbor seals cruising by. The Salmon Wellington is probably the best of its kind anywhere.

Again, this is a place where the wines are plentiful and thoughtfully chosen and where the seafood is fresh as can be (one of the coast's leading suppliers is just a few doors down the road). The place is humming, especially on weekends and in the summer, and when one of Peter Burge's customized oyster platters is on the fresh sheet, it's where I tend to go first.

Accompaniment
Big starch

Wine
Rodney Strong
California
Chardonnay

12 medium oysters
Oil for sautéing
Salt and pepper
2 cups / 500 mL tomato sauce
   (your own favorite recipe or a good
   commercial one)
2 oz. / 60 g thinly sliced pancetta,
   julienned
½ lb. / 250 g bocconcini, sliced into
   ⅛" / 30 mm rounds
2 cups / 500 mL béchamel sauce
4 Tbsp. / 60 mL parmesan cheese, grated

Sauté oysters in a small amount of oil over high heat, about 2 minutes. Season lightly with salt and pepper. Lightly butter the bottoms of 4 individual baking dishes, or use one large one. Divide tomato sauce among dishes. Place oysters on top of sauce. Sprinkle on pancetta. Layer on bocconcini, béchamel and grated parmesan. Bake 20 minutes in center of oven at 425°F (220°C).

Béchamel Sauce
   4 Tbsp. / 60 mL butter
   3 Tbsp. / 45 mL all-purpose flour
   1½ cups / 375 mL milk
   Pinch ground nutmeg
   Salt and white pepper to taste

Melt butter in a saucepan. Add the flour and cook, stirring, over low heat for 3 minutes. Raise heat to medium and slowly add the milk, stirring constantly with a wire whisk. Continue whisking until sauce thickens, about 5 minutes. Add the nutmeg, salt and white pepper.

Serves 4.

STEWS

They're fun to make—
easy and flexible, creative,
expandable to accommodate
any number of eaters.

Kate's Lazom

Lazom is merely an acronym for the main ingredients: lamb, avocado, zucchini and oyster mushrooms. This is a "zipstew," and that's my term for one that tastes as though you've spent two days on it. This inspiration was partly my wife, Kate's.

This may be a good point to do the disclaimer/reclaimer I meant to do at the start. It is assumed—as the Atlantic Monthly's *cryptopuzzlers always stated, and I'm paraphrasing due to faulty memory—that you know how to cook and understand portions. I'm not sure I do, either of them. Writing recipes is all but impossible for me—as it is for most people who cook, so I'm told—without having a home economist or a professional cookbook compiler follow me around with a bunch of measuring spoons and cups and a tape recorder.*

The lamb is crucial, of course. If you know someone who raises it, there's your source. If you have a good butcher, trust him or her. Otherwise, a couple of names to know are Howard at Windsor Meats in West Van and Linda at Edgemont Meats in North Van. Failing that, places with "organic meat" sections are worth frequenting.

A few slices of good bacon

A couple of hefty garlic cloves with no spots

4 or 5 firm shallots (beware those mushy ones you find in some supermarkets)

1 lb. / 500 g chunk of fresh lamb (leg, roast) without much fat on it

Coarse black pepper (no salt; there's usually enough in the stock unless you use the low-sodium variety; anyway, let your palate judge but don't put any in until later)

Beef broth or stock and red wine, enough to create stewishness (or chicken broth or stock and white wine: depending on stock/wine, the color of the stew and the flavors change; chicken is lighter, beef heartier; both work equally well)

A handful of sun-dried tomatoes (dry, not the packed-in-oil kind), crumbled

Some oyster mushrooms (fresh are nice but canned are just fine)

Fresh thyme stripped from the stems

Chopped parsley

A big ripe (but not mushy) avocado

A big juicy lemon

A couple of small, firm zucchinis

Dice, then sauté the bacon until most of the fat's rendered, reserving the bacon bits and the fat separately. Chop, then sauté garlic and shallots in a little of the fat and reserve.

Cut lamb in stew-sized cubes and brown well in more fat, adding a little oil if needed. Pepper the lamb cubes liberally. Add stock and wine of choice. Sprinkle in sun-dried tomatoes. Add thyme and parsley.

Over medium-high heat, let some of the liquid reduce. Simmer covered for 15 to 20 minutes until the lamb has the tenderness you like; don't let it get rubbery.

Meanwhile peel and cube avocado and sprinkle with lemon juice and reserve. Slice (and peel if desired) and cube the zucchini. Cut oyster mushrooms into manageable pieces.

Five minutes before it's all done add zucchini and mushrooms to stew, stir to mix, and continue simmering.

One minute before it's all done add avocado with its lemon juice to stew, stirring to mix. Take off heat and let sit for 5 minutes with the lid on.

Serve in big heated bowls. Sprinkle with bacon bits. Add a dollop of sour cream on top if you're so inclined.

Try it for 2 and then expand to feed 4 or more.

Accompaniment
Peppered focaccia bread or Portuguese mealy buns; red pepper jelly and Winnipeg cream cheese on Ak-Mak crackers (appetizer); shredded green and red cabbage with cracked black pepper and freshly grated ginger and chopped scallions, with oil-and-vinegar-and-dry-mustard dressing to which you've added 1/4 teaspoon of poppy seeds; sliced ripe nectarines with brown sugar and sour cream; puréed cherries with kirsch and pine nut meringues.

Wine
The same color as you used in the stock

84

Dinner and a Ride Home for Cinderella: Stew in a Pumpkin

I've been making this for so long I'm surprised people still want to eat it, me included. Mid-October is the one time of the year when this can be made with all fresh ingredients, if you're lucky and have a good market close by.

Its origin is somewhere in South America and like many such, it has undergone considerable transformation. There are also endless variations on it, certainly with herbs and seasonings, but essential are (A) good meat (beef is best but lamb works too); (B) good corn; (C) good peaches (all right, nectarines aren't bad—they stay firmer—but don't use dried peaches no matter how organic or sunny).

It's a favorite for company; no point doing it up for just the two of you unless you want to be eating it for a week. It's a fair bit of work, though I did once, in a moment of culinary masochism, prepare it in six individual little pumpkins. Now I can only play New Age music on the piano . . .

A firm, fresh pumpkin is essential. It's the tureen, you see. Buy two—one for the stew and one for the porch. The one you cook will eventually collapse inward, leaving a face only Chas. Addams could love.

Accompaniment
Crusty French bread and lots of it; quince jelly with Münster cheese; a lot of cold grapes

Wine
Errazuriz Merlot from Chile; Parducci Zinfandel from California; Lang's Pinot Meunier from Naramata; a cool glass of Taylor's Chip Dry White Port; Graham's Six Grapes after

The Stew
3 lbs. / 1.5 kg lean beef, cut into
   1″ / 2.5 cm cubes
½ cup / 125 mL good olive oil
   (extra virgin oil from Argentina in the
   triangular bottle would be terribly
   authentic!)
2 large onions, chopped
3 large green peppers, chopped
4-5 cloves garlic, chopped
2 tsp. / 10 mL salt, more or less as
   needed
1 tsp. / 5 mL black pepper, more or less
   as needed
2 large bay leaves
3-4 Tbsp. / 45-60 mL tomato paste, more
   if you like it darker
2 tsp. / 10 mL fresh thyme
   (or 1 tsp. / 5 mL dried)
2 cups / 500 mL robust red wine
   (zinfandel is nice)
1 cup / 250 mL beef broth, or enough to
   keep everything submerged as it
   cooks
2 cups / 500 mL squash cut into
   1″ / 2.5 cm cubes
2 cups / 500 mL fresh green beans
2 cups / 500 mL carrots cut into
   ½″ / 1.5 cm cubes or rounds
2 cups / 500 mL cabbage (the big
   crunchy outside leaves) chopped in
   big pieces
1 lb. / 500 g fresh ripe tomatoes
(or a 16-oz. / 455 mL can, chopped)
3 cobs corn (or 2 cups / 500 mL kernels)
6-8 fresh peaches, peeled, pitted and
   halved

Brown meat in hot oil, a few pieces at a time, placing them in a big casserole with a lid as they brown. Add onions, peppers and garlic to remaining oil 'n' drippings. Stir over medium heat until onions get to that transcendental state cookbooks always talk about: translucent, soft but not brown. Take it all out with a slotted spoon, including the gludge on the bottom, and add to the pot where the meat is.

Set low heat under the casserole, stirring in salt and pepper, bay leaves, tomato paste, thyme. Add wine, stir well, turn heat up and cover the pot. Cook for 10 to 15 minutes.

Add beef broth, stirring up all the gludge from the bottom, and bring to a simmer. Cover again and put the casserole in 325°F (160°C) oven.

Take a look in 15 minutes or so and adjust temperature so it just keeps a steady, easy simmer—no megaboiling. Cook for 1 hour, then check the meat for tenderness; you want it tender but not falling apart. You may have to cook it 10 or 15 minutes more.

Add all the vegetables except the corn, cover again and continue cooking 15 to 20 minutes—you want the veggies tender too, but not mush. Add the corn and the peaches and cook 10 minutes. Check for salt, pepper and thyme, adding more if needed.

Take it out of the oven and keep warm or refrigerate covered until tomorrow.

The Pumpkin
　1 10"-diameter / 25 cm pumpkin,
　　or bigger
　Milk

Cut a good-sized lid off the top of the pumpkin, keeping the stalk on for a good handle. Scrape out all the seeds and fibers but watch that you don't scrape a hole in the side or the bottom of the pumpkin. Rinse the pumpkin well a couple of times with milk, discard the milk and sprinkle a little salt and pepper inside. Put the pumpkin, opening up, on a baking dish in a 350°F (180°C) oven.

Cook for 45 minutes and check for softness. You want the flesh tender enough to scrape into the stew but you don't want the walls of the pumpkin to collapse. It may take another 15 to 20 minutes of baking, depending on size. You can cook the lid in the oven too but it will be done much quicker and will shrink and fall into the pumpkin, so just put it in for the last 15 to 20 minutes.

Ladle stew gently into the pumpkin. Don't pour it all in at once—it'll split the tureen and get all over you and everything.

Scrape out a little pumpkin flesh when you serve the stew. Again, be careful!

The pumpkin is a one-shot bowl, but the stew reheats wonderfully.

Serves a bunch.

Hershey Chili with Christmas Spices and Nuts (Plus a Red Chili Apple Pie After)

Driving through New Mexico turned up a lot of good things—big bags of chili powder in varying strengths to take home; posters and sculptures; a really nice scarf (it was winter); a wooden crate of Santa Fe Pale Ale and a lot of surprising wine. I didn't know that New Mexico had the oldest wine industry on the continent either. There were wonderful meals, from the elaborate at Santacafe to the homey at Marie Ysabel's. Chili is the heart and soul of northern New Mexico cooking and even finds its way into what's called New New Mexico Mexican(!) although milk chocolate in your chili and red chili in your apple pie aren't old standards. Tasty, though. The chocolate chili reheats nicely. The apple pie does not and must be eaten warm out of the oven.

Accompaniment
Rice, tortillas, polenta

Wine
Santa Fe Pale Ale or New Mexico champagne

1 medium can pinto beans
4 cups / 1 L water
2 Tbsp. / 25 mL lard
1 Tbsp. / 15 mL bacon fat
2 onions, coarsely chopped
5 cloves garlic, crushed
1 lb. / 500 g chorizo or Italian hot or Nürnberger bratwurst sausage, pricked with a fork and simmered in hot water for 15 minutes
1 lb. / 500 g lean beef, chili-chopped or coarsely ground
1 tsp. / 5 mL anise seeds
1 tsp. / 5 mL crushed coriander seeds
1 tsp. / 5 mL fennel seeds
½ tsp. / 2 mL ground cloves
½ tsp. / 2 mL ground cinnamon
1 tsp. / 5 mL freshly ground black pepper
1 tsp. / 5 mL paprika
1 tsp. / 5 mL ground nutmeg
1 tsp. / 5 mL ground cumin
2 tsp. / 10 mL oregano
1 doz. whole dried red chilies, crushed and softened in hot water, then drained
1 small can tomato paste
2½ Tbsp. / 35 mL vinegar
3 Tbsp. / 45 mL lemon juice
1 small milk chocolate Hershey Bar broken into pieces (or a handful of Hershey kisses)
2 small fresh tortillas, chopped into 1" / 2.5 cm pieces
5 Tbsp. / 75 mL sesame seeds, black or white
1 cup / 250 mL crushed almonds

Put beans and their liquid in a big pot. Pour in 2½ to 3 cups (600 to 750 mL) more water. Bring to a boil over medium heat. Lower heat and simmer, partly covered, until beans are cooked but not mushy. You may need to add more water while the beans cook. Drain beans and reserve the liquid.

Melt lard in frying pan and add the beans. Fry lightly for 3 or 4 minutes. Set aside. Melt bacon fat in a big pot over medium heat. Add onions and garlic and cook 'til soft.

Slice the sausage thin or cut into cubes (or crumble if it's the Italian) and add the beef and the anise seeds, coriander, fennel seeds, cloves, cinnamon, black pepper, paprika, nutmeg, cumin and oregano. Put the meats and spices mixture into the pot with the onion. Brown, stirring periodically, until meat is well browned.

Pour the rest of the bean cooking water into the pot and add everything else, except the beans. Bring to a boil, lower heat and cook with lid off for 30 minutes. Add the beans and simmer another 30 minutes. Stir occasionally, adding water if the mixture looks to be getting too thick and dry.

Serve when you get hungry; the chili can simmer on very low for a long time.

Serves 4.

Apple Chili Pie

87

5 cups / 1.25 L peeled and sliced apples
1 cup / 250 mL sugar
2 Tbsp. / 25 mL butter
1 tsp. / 5 mL cinnamon
½ tsp. / 2 mL nutmeg
2½ tsp. / 12 mL red chili powder
1 cup / 250 mL water
Dash salt
1 unbaked 9" (23 cm) pie shell with
 top crust

Combine everything (except pie shell) in a big pot and cook on medium heat for 20 minutes. Pour mixture into unbaked pie shell and dot with extra butter. Pat crust on top. Bake 35 to 40 minutes at 375°F (190°C) or until crust is brown.

Kraut Kraut (A Choucroute for All Seasons)

Accompaniment

Endive and escarole salad with lox (the Jewish deli kind, not the West Coast smoked salmon variety) and a little foie gras dressed with nut oil, vinegar, mustard, garlic. Boiled potatoes (not mushy) with snipped chives. Münster cheese with caraway seeds on the side and lots of crusty bread. Fresh fruit for dessert, with cream.

Wine

Kronenbourg beer first, then Trimbach Pinot Blanc, followed by Ostertag Gewürztraminer, followed by some iced eau de vie. Bed, nearby.

Choucroute garni is what they call it—another innocuous, generic name for such a fabulous food—garnished sauerkraut. It hardly hints at the gustatory pleasures of such a platter; sauerkraut's only the half of it. In Alsace it is practically the national dish. It's served all the time, any time. For me, autumn is the best time to cook it. It takes a little doing, rounding up all the meats and the mustards—to say nothing of a like-minded group of eaters to share it with.

Since choucroute is based on sauerkraut, the briny cabbage is crucial to its success. Some homemade is too bland, some commercial, too salty. You have to experiment until you find your taste—midway between biting and soft.

At least 10 mustards are required to accompany choucroute: German Düsseldorfer; English hot; grainy cider; sweet Russian; one with herbs (my favorite is packed by Harrod's, with nettle leaves); smoky or mesquite; spicy, with jalapeños perhaps; plain old French's ballpark; freshly made from dry Keen's; Dijon, of course; more if you're so inclined. Plus those tiny cornichons, all crunchy and salty.

And at least six kinds of sausages: bratwurst, kielbasa, weisswurst, debreciner, garlic ring, Mennonite. I also like blood sausage in the mix. It tends to disintegrate but a good German variety will impart a very herby marjoram-savory taste to the surrounding sauerkraut. You also need some smoked pork loin, called Kassler.

It all reheats handsomely, especially the sauerkraut in the juices.

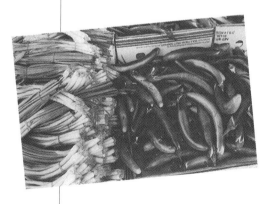

4-5 lbs. / 1.75-2.25 kg sauerkraut

½ lb. / 250 g smoked lean bacon,
    cut in strips

3 large onions, chopped

4 cloves garlic, peeled and quartered or
    mashed flat

1 tsp. / 5 mL cumin seeds (start with
    that and add more to taste)

10-12 juniper berries, bruised with knife

3 cloves

2 big bay leaves

A few sprigs fresh thyme (or crumbled,
    dry)

1 tsp. / 5 mL each salt and pepper,
    or to taste

Sausages galore, cut into pieces or left
    whole depending on how messy you
    want to get

½-¾" / 1.5-2 cm smoked pork loin
    chops (Kassler), 1 per guest

1½ lb. / 750 g slab good meaty bacon,
    all in a piece

1 lb. / 500 g dried pears cut into
    ½" / 1.5 cm strips

2 cups / 500 mL semidry white wine
    (riesling or gewürztraminer)

1-2 cups / 250-500 mL chicken or veal
    stock

5-8 Tbsp. / 75-120 mL kirsch (use gin if
    you don't want to buy a bottle of
    kirsch)

Soak sauerkraut 20 minutes in cold water, drain, rinse and squeeze as dry as possible. In a big pan cook bacon 'til semi-crunchy. Pour off some of the fat and, over low heat, cook onions and garlic covered for 15 minutes.

Add garlic and onions to sauerkraut. Stir in cumin seeds, juniper berries, cloves, bay leaves, thyme, salt and pepper. Mix thoroughly. Heat oven to 350°F (180°C). Spread an inch or so (2.5 cm) of sauerkraut on the bottom of a very big casserole (it has to hold a lot). Add a layer of meats and throw on some dried pears. More sauerkraut and keep layering 'til everything's in the pot and you can still get the lid on. Pour in wine and stock. Stir as much as you are able. Bring to boil over high heat. Cover casserole and put it in the oven. Cook 30 to 45 minutes (start checking for doneness after 30; don't overcook).

Bring it out, add kirsch or gin and maybe more wine if it looks too dry, and cook in oven another 10 minutes. Let cool for a few minutes and then pour into heated serving bowl or onto individual plates.

Pour more wine, make sure there's lots of bread; prepare yourself for adulation.

Serves 6 or 1.

Cioppino: A Dish for Consenting Adults

It's a runny stew or a fat soup and it's not Italian. Rather it was probably first devised by some Mediterranean fishing type who got homesick and couldn't find anything comparable in California so went out and cooked his own. People who eat this have to know each other pretty well—well enough to concentrate on the food. This is not a dinner prelude for romantic liaisons; this is a dinner prelude to a brisk nap. This one can be made a day ahead if you stop preparation just before adding the seafood. About an hour before you want to eat, pick it up from "Meanwhile scrub the clams and mussels . . . " Three bottles of wine are required: one for the chef while cooking, one for the pot, one for the table. Maybe four.

Veggies
¼ cup / 50 mL good olive oil

5-6 medium onions, chopped chunky

10 cloves good garlic, peeled and chopped

3 medium red peppers, seeded and chopped

2 medium green peppers, seeded and chopped

5 ribs celery and leaves, chopped

1 bunch fresh fennel, fronds and bulb, chopped

3-4 medium zucchinis, chopped chunky

1 bottle Parducci California Zinfandel (you can use other people's Zin but don't use any other kind of wine)

8 cups / 2 L fish stock

2 lbs. / 1 kg ripe roma tomatoes, seeded and quartered

Seasonings
8-10 basil leaves, or 2 Tbsp. / 25 mL dried, chopped

½ tsp. / 2 mL fennel seeds

2-3 bay leaves

Salt and lots of fresh black pepper

Chili pepper flakes (optional)

Fish Stuff
1 doz. each clams, mussels (feel free to use more) and prawns (or double amount of shrimp)

1 whole crab, disassembled

1 bunch fresh parsley, chopped

1 lb. / 500 g halibut, in chunks

¾ cup / 175 mL good olive oil

The Rest

- 2-3 slices white bread
- 2 jalapeños, seeded and chopped
- More garlic, to taste
- ½ cup / 125 mL good olive oil
- 24 slices very thin French bread, oven-toasted, cooled and rubbed with garlic cloves

Heat about ¼ cup (50 mL) of the oil in a deep pan or wok. Add onions and garlic and cook 10 minutes over medium heat. Add peppers, celery and fennel and zucchini and cook another 10. Transfer everything to a big warm pot.

Pour in the bottle of zinfandel . . . yes, all of it. Pour in a similar amount of fish stock. Add tomatoes, then the seasonings, plus salt and pepper to taste. Stir well, up the heat and let it boil properly, once. Simmer partly covered for 20 minutes. Check seasonings.

Meanwhile scrub the clams and mussels thoroughly and put in another pot with a little water. Steam, covered, on high heat until they open. Reserve.

Soak the white bread slices in a little water and squeeze dry. Pound bread and jalapeños and some garlic into a paste. Add ½ cup oil (125 mL), a very small trickle at a time, as if making mayonnaise. Add a couple of spoonfuls of fish stock and some salt and pepper.

Bring cioppino to another boil and add prawns or shrimp plus crab, clams and mussels (in their shells).

Add lots of chopped parsley. Adjust liquid (stock and/or wine) as needed. Heat it all through. Add halibut and heat another 3 minutes. Take cioppino off heat, collect yourself and set the tureen before four or five people, six if restrained, three if piggy.

Serve the little garlicky toasts with the garlic-oil-pepper spread you made in the mortar. You can put it in the bottom of a bowl and pour the stew over it or eat alongside. Roll up your sleeves and get down and messy. Serves three to six consenting adults.

Accompaniment
Much more bread

Wine
Zinfandel

92

Bollito misto con salsa verde

Gildo Casadei,
Bianco Nero Ristorante, Vancouver

What a drab term for such a marvellous meal: "boiled mixed meats," hardly giving a clue to the tasty treats this pot of stewed meat offers up. There's also "fried mixed," a batter-coated, crispy-critter version that sometimes has fish in it as well. Both have been prepared for me by master chef Gildo Casadei over the years. I think the boiled is my favorite. A thick, garlicky green sauce is the perfect accompaniment.

Few of us have ready access to a calf's head and even if we did, who'd be prepared to let it simmer away in the kitchen? Someone might inadvertently lift the lid and—yikes! So the chef suggests using lots and lots of veal bones, with as much meat left on them as possible. Don't leave out the beef tongue, though. It's a particular treat chilled, sliced thin and served with horseradish mayonnaise.

Cotechino sausage is another of the cornerstones of this dish. A good Italian butcher or deli can supply it for you.

Accompaniment
More boiled potatoes; Tuscan bread for dipping; a little grilled radicchio and melted mozzarella over oyster mushrooms

Wine
Dolcetto d'Alba

Bollito misto
1 cotechino sausage
1 beef tongue
1 piece beef brisket
1 calf's head (if unavailable, use lots of veal bones)
1 chicken
1 stalk celery
2 carrots
1 leek
3 potatoes
Much parsley, chopped
Kosher salt
Cracked black peppercorns

Prick the cotechino with a fork, boil for 2 hours and set aside. Boil beef tongue separately (about 1 hour per pound or half-kilogram) and set aside. Cook beef brisket in boiling water for 1 hour. Add calf's head and cook for 30 minutes. Add chicken and vegetables and cook for 30 minutes. Add cotechino and cook for 5 to 10 minutes more. Throw in lots and lots of chopped parsley. Heat through. Salt and pepper to taste.

Salsa verde
4 Tbsp. / 60 mL finely chopped parsley
2 anchovy fillets, finely chopped
1 piece of bread, crust cut off, soaked in vinegar, squeezed dry
Extra virgin olive oil
Plenty of chopped garlic
Salt and cracked black peppercorns

Combine parsley, anchovy, bread and mix well. Add olive oil, garlic, salt and pepper and beat well to make a sauce. Spoon over meats, or use as dip.

Serves 4, 6 if they're Presbyterian.

VEGGIES

*Vegetables should get
as much attention as
any aspect of a meal.*

Sweet and Bitter Greens with Roasted Beet And Shallot Vinaigrette

Monique A. Barbeau, *Fullers Restaurant, Sheraton Seattle Hotel and Towers*

Accompaniment
Bread sticks, lavash; seedy-bread toast; just about anything

Wine
No. Maybe a dry cider.

Monique is one of the great chefs. Don't just take my word for it because that's what the world is telling her too. Helping Fullers Restaurant in the downtown Seattle Sheraton regain its top star recently, she also shared the Best Chef in the Pacific Northwest award with another skilled and creative Seattle cook, Tom Douglas, ex-Dahlia Lounge, more recently of Etta's Seafood.

As for Fullers, it's one of those North American relative-rarities, a superb restaurant-in-a-hotel. Europe and Asia seem to have that thing down a lot patter than we. Here, how often do we say, "Oh, we'll just eat in the hotel tonight!"

Well, just you try it as an afterthought at Fullers; chances are you won't get in unless you've booked weeks ahead. It's small and cozy and the food, under Monique's direction, is state of the art. And the wine list is great and, and, and . . .

I think the fact that this is one of her big signature dishes is a perfect indicator of the kind of culinary iconoclast she is.

Imagine—a salad. Most chefs would make it meat or a fabulous fish; maybe a killer-caloric dessert. She does salad. (Of course, Fullers is a no-smoking restaurant too, so innovation isn't anything new here.)

Yes, it's a lot more work than the average salad. Yes, it's well worth it. Yes, it's even better if you go there and have her make one up for you.

Vinaigrette
1 doz. beets, peeled
1 doz. shallots, whole
Olive oil
Splash white wine
⅓ cup / 75 mL vinegar
½ cup / 125 mL salad oil
½ cup / 125 mL olive oil

Coat beets and shallots with olive oil and a splash of wine. Roast in oven until tender. Purée. This base should be thick.

Add vinegar to the puréed base in the blender and incorporate. Slowly add the oils to incorporate into an emulsion. Season with salt and freshly ground white pepper, to taste.

Greens (and Reds)
   1 large beet
   1 large shallot
   Variety of sweet and bitter lettuces for
     4-6 servings
   4-6 radicchio lettuce "cups"

Peel and cut beet into thin strips about matchstick size. Coat thoroughly but lightly with all-purpose flour. Deep-fry until strips lose their moisture. Drain on paper towel. Season with salt. Set aside.

Slice shallot into thin rings and separate. Proceed as with beets.

Place a small handful of greens in a bowl. Add about 2 Tbsp. (30 mL) dressing. Use salt and freshly ground white pepper to taste. Toss completely. On a plate, place radicchio as a cup and fill with dressed greens. Garnish with fried beets and shallots.

Serves 4 to 6.

Emily's Brother Tom's Famous Sauerkraut Salad from Wolf Lake, Illinois

Dr. Emily Goetz, Vancouver

Accompaniment
Wild duck breast
(halved, marinated in
soy and Worcester-
shire sauce and
broiled with butter,
7 minutes on one
side, 5 on the other
for medium rare, and
sprinkled with black
pepper); boiled
potatoes with chives;
Gelato Fresco

Wine
Guigal Côtes du
Rhône; Mirassou
Petite Sirah

DiscDrive *listeners respond to a lot of my musings and ramblings. I once made some reference to Mozart having bought high-tops that made his feet hurt and someone from the Bata Shoe Museum wanted to get more details! More people have asked me about this sauerkraut salad than just about any concoction I chatted about in 1992. This came about on the occasion of "Official Sauerkraut Salad Week." I made reference to the fact I had (A) never heard of such a thing as sauer-kraut salad, let alone tasted it; and (B) wasn't sure such a celebration existed. Response was swift. "The salad exists!" insisted the correspondent who appended her brother Tom's recipe. I ran through the ingredients lickety-split one afternoon on the air and that's when the barrage began. "We want this recipe," people demanded from all over the country and I photo-copied hundreds and sent them away. For anybody who missed it, here it is again. I just can't remember when sauerkraut salad week is . . .*

4 cups / 1 L sauerkraut
½ onion, chopped
½ green pepper, chopped
Pimento, to taste, chopped
6 Tbsp. / 90 mL yellow sandwich mustard
4-6 Tbsp. / 60-90 mL prepared horseradish
1 tsp. dry mustard powder
Caraway seed, to taste

Mix everything and chill. Serves 4.

Shiitake Mushrooms with Okra and Corn

Rich or what? Don't even look at this if you and your doctor don't see eye-to-eye on the subject of cream and cheese. As a side dish for simple grilled meats or fish, it's wonderful. If you use vegetable stock instead of chicken, it's glorious as a vegetarian dish. Michael Roberts of Trumps in L.A. used to serve something similar he called risotto, even though there wasn't any rice in it, because of the texture the corn gives it. In my copy of his book he wrote, "Eating well is the best revenge." I try.

½ cup / 125 mL unsalted butter
3 big summer corncobs, kernels
    stripped off, about 3 cups / 750 mL
3 Tbsp. / 45 mL minced shallots
1 cup / 250 mL chicken stock
1 cup / 250 mL whipping cream
½ cup / 125 mL grated parmesan
1 doz. fresh okra (or 1 small pkg.
    frozen—thawed, well-drained, rinsed)
1 doz. shiitake mushrooms, caps only
Salt and pepper to taste

Put oven on to warm. Put ¼ cup (50 mL) of the butter in a pot over medium heat and melt. Add corn and shallots and cook 2 to 3 minutes. Add ½ cup (125 mL) of the stock and raise heat to high. Reduce liquid, 5 to 7 minutes.

Add cream, reduce again 7 to 8 minutes until thick. Remove from heat and add cheese. Transfer everything to a blender or food processor and pulse to just break up the corn. Don't purée. Remove to a bowl and keep warm in the oven.

Put the rest of the butter in a pan over medium. When hot add okra and mushrooms and cook 4 to 5 minutes, stirring all the time. Add remainder of stock and cook until thickened. Add salt and pepper.

Bring corn out of the oven. Arrange mushrooms and okra on top, and pour all the juices over.

Serves 6.

Accompaniment
Plain buttered noodles sprinkled with 1 teaspoon poppyseed; mustard green and escarole salad; rare-grilled lamb loin with vinaigrette

Wine
Cool valpolicella or beaujolais; Spanish or Chilean sparkling wine

Vegetable Hash with Basil Pesto

Tina Perenseff for
Bishop's Restaurant, Vancouver

Tina used to cook at lunchtime in John Bishop's excellent restaurant, and, sitting with my publisher there one day, he buying and all, I opted for this dish which I liked so much I finally persuaded Tina to let me have it for my own edification and now, yours. I never fail to credit her though and neither should you.

Hash

½ cup / 125 mL eggplant, roasted and brunoise*
½ cup / 125 mL bell pepper, brunoise
½ cup / 125 mL zucchini, brunoise
½ cup / 125 mL fresh tomato, concasse**
1 Tbsp. / 15 mL black olives, chopped
1 Tbsp. / 15 mL sun-dried tomatoes, chopped
3 Tbsp. / 45 mL basil pesto

* brunoise: vegetables cut into tiny cubes about ⅛" / 3 mm a side
**concasse: peeled, seeded tomatoes cut into tiny cubes about ⅛" / 3 mm a side

To roast eggplant: slice in half down the center lengthwise. Rub each side with vegetable oil. Roast at 350°F (189°C) until tender.

Sauté all vegetable ingredients in 1 Tbsp. (15 mL) vegetable oil. Add pesto to mixture when vegetables are tender. Heat through.

Pesto

1 lb. / 500 g fresh basil leaves
5 garlic cloves
3 Tbsp. / 45 mL pine nuts, toasted
1 Tbsp. / 15 mL coarse salt
1 cup / 250 mL grated parmesan cheese
1 cup / 250 mL virgin olive oil

Wash and dry basil leaves. Put all ingredients except olive oil in a food processor or blender. Blend mixture into paste. Gently work in the olive oil until smooth.

If you plan to freeze the pesto, leave out the cheese and add it at serving time, 1 part cheese to 4 parts pesto.

Four servings hash, 1 quart (1 L) pesto.

Accompaniment
A poached egg on top of the hash; oven-toasted bread slices; chicken-stock-cooked arborio rice

Wine
Something in the Sonoma sauvignon blanc line

Irio

Amyn Sunderji, *Kilimanjaro Restaurant, Vancouver*

Amyn's restaurant has been recognized as unique by everybody from the New York Times *to* Western Living. *Here you can sit and tuck into delightful, delicious treats. Here was the first place I ate ostrich. Here's the occasional rare bottle of red wine stacked in the cellar that can be coaxed out to join your party. Here's fun with your food and hearty flavors with sublime seasoning.*

 4 medium potatoes
 1 bunch spinach leaves, chopped
 ½ cup / 125 mL cilantro, chopped
 1 tsp. / 5 mL coarse black pepper,
     or to taste
 ½ tsp. / 2 mL salt, or to taste
 Juice of ½ lemon
 ¼ cup / 50 mL light whipping cream
 Parsley for garnish

Boil and peel potatoes. Blanch spinach and chop coarsely. In a bowl, mix all the ingredients, mashing the potatoes with a fork. Serve hot, mounded on a plate, as a side dish. Garnish with parsley sprig.

"This recipe is a variation of the traditional side dish called meru, by the people of Kenya," says the chef over a frosty bottle of Tusker Lager. "Yams or cassava or other tubers can be used, with taro leaves or collard greens."

Serves 4.

99

Accompaniment
Prawns piri piri; filet of ostrich

Wine
Stanley E&E Black Pepper Shiraz, or Château Musar from Lebanon

Beans, Pears and Bacon (Bohnen, Birnen und Speck)

This is one of the few dishes I remember—and still like—from my childhood in Berlin. There's nothing crisp or al dente about these green beans—they're cooked! The pears get mushy, which is the way they're supposed to be. In Hamburg you get this as a side dish with just about anything. For years I tried to figure out what "beanweed" (bohnenkraut) was; it gives this and many other German dishes a distinctive flavor. It's savory—plain old summer savory, though I'm still convinced the German strain has a slightly wilder edge of flavor. Thyme can take its place in the recipe, just this once. You can try it as a vegetarian dish (Bohnen und Birnen, ohne Speck!) by using a rich vegetable stock instead of plain water and adding some more herbs (fresh marjoram, chives, sorrel, a little arugula).

½ l / 125 mL cup water

½ tsp. / 2 mL salt

1 lb. / 500 g green beans, ends snipped, snapped into 2" / 5 cm pieces

1 lb. / 500 g ripe but not mushy pears, peeled cored and cut into small cubes

½ lb. / 250 g speck (lean smoked German bacon), cubed about ½" / 1.5 cm

1 Tbsp. / 15 mL fresh summer savory, chopped
(or ½ tsp. / 2 mL dried and crumbled)

½ tsp. / 2 mL black pepper

3 Tbsp. / 45 mL parsley, chopped

Bring water and salt to a boil in a big pot. Reduce heat and put in the beans. Add pear and bacon cubes on top. Sprinkle with savory and pepper. Simmer covered over very low heat for about an hour (check after 50 minutes to make sure the mixture isn't totally disintegrating—the key here is very, very low, steady heat). Add parsley, toss to mix and serve at once.

Serves 4.

Accompaniment
Sourdough rye bread; steamed potatoes *salzkartoffeln* style (boil to desired doneness, drain, add a little salt and a quarter stick of butter, return to heat and shake over flame for about 60 seconds—don't forget the crumbly buttery bits at the bottom—they're the best part)

Wine
Berliner Kindl beer for me, or St. Pauli Girl or Beck's; a halbtrocken riesling from the Mosel

Spicy Green Beans and Carrots

It's strange to recall now, but my first experience with Ethiopian cooking came in Washington D.C. at a hole-in-the-wall restaurant. I doubt if it's still operating; at least I haven't been back there in well over a decade to find out. Vegetable stews of all kinds are a standard item on Ethiopian menus. The taste of the butter is rich and nutty, the spices add a level of heat you can temper to suit your own tongue and tummy.

1 lb. / 500 g fresh green beans,
   ends snipped, snapped into
   2" / 5 cm pieces
Oil for sautéing
1 large onion, chopped
Jalapeño peppers (1 or more), seeded
   and chopped
3 medium garlic cloves, chopped
3 tsp. / 15 mL peeled and chopped fresh
   ginger
1 tsp. / 5 mL Hungarian paprika
Cayenne pepper to taste
½ tsp. / 2 mL cinnamon
¼ tsp. / 1 mL cloves
½ tsp. / 2 mL turmeric
Pinch freshly grated nutmeg
1 lb. / 500 g carrots, quartered and cut
   into 2" / 5 cm lengths
Salt to taste
1½ / 375 mL cups cold water
2 Tbsp. / 25 mL tomato paste
Green onions, chopped
Plain yogurt

Fill large pan with salted water and boil. Add beans and boil 3 minutes. Drain and rinse with cold water.

In a big pan, heat oil and add onion. Cook over medium heat for 10 minutes or 'til golden. Add jalapeños, garlic, ginger, all the spices and cook on low for 2 to 3 minutes. Add carrots and salt. Add 1 cup (250 mL) of the water and bring to simmer. Cover the pan and cook on low for 10 to 12 minutes.

Add tomato paste mixed with a little water. Heat through. Add more water if needed, though sauce should be quite thick. If too thin, take lid off and simmer for a couple of minutes. Add the beans to the sauce and heat through.

Garnish with chopped green onions and a dollop of yogurt on each serving.

Serves 4.

Accompaniment
Ethiopian cold flatbreads (the ones that look like uncooked pancakes), warm rice

Wine
Dry cider or beer; fresh mango *lassi*

Armagnac Leeks and Green Beans

I'll confess to luring you into this recipe with promises of my favorite brandy; a cheap trick, admittedly, since there is no Armagnac in this pot of beans. The dish comes from the region, that's all. Nothing, however, says you can't add some just before serving if you see a window of opportunity; then perhaps you can light the whole dish on fire—why should only meat and desserts get all that flamboyant glory? If you double up on the ham and the egg and the vinegar, it's virtually a meal. This way I use it as a side dish for a hearty barbecued fish or some chicken or pork.

Accompaniment
Slow-simmered ribs; confit of goose; roast chicken

Wine
Some of that nicely raunchy light red they grow in Gascony; Barossa Valley rosé; Sumac Ridge Okanagan Blush

1½ lbs. / 750 g green beans, the thinner the better
3-4 leeks, the white and about 1½" / 4 cm of the green, split
2 cloves garlic, minced
Salt and white pepper to taste
2 Tbsp. / 25 mL olive oil (or rendered bacon fat or goose fat, if you're in Armagnac country)
2 medium onions, chopped
3 slices ham, diced
2 Tbsp. / 25 mL flour
1 egg yolk
1 tsp. / 5 mL white wine vinegar
Parsley, tarragon, sorrel, chopped

Bring a pot of salted water to the boil. Throw in beans, leeks and garlic. Boil 8 to 10 minutes. Drain vegetables, reserving 1 cup (250 mL) cooking water.

In a skillet, heat oil or fat and sauté onions and ham together over medium, for 8 to 10 minutes. Stir in the flour and cook, then pour in the reserved cooking water. Stir constantly over medium heat until the sauce is smooth. Add vegetables and simmer gently, 8 to 10 minutes. Remove from heat and put lid on skillet.

Beat egg yolk and vinegar together.

Beat a little of the hot sauce into the egg mixture, then pour it all into the skillet with the beans. Heat through until sauce thickens, but don't let it boil again.

Garnish with herbs.

Serves 4.

Münstered Potatoes

Münster cheese isn't always easy to find in Canada, and when it is you usually know it—from a distance. As with most of the world's great smelly cheeses, aroma and flavor are two different things. Danish Esrom works here, in a pinch.

1 big Yukon Gold potato, baked
2 oz. / 50 mL ripe Münster cheese,
   rind removed
Black pepper

Scrub the potato well, dry, rub all over with butter, and bake on rack in hot oven for 20 minutes. Then prick with a fork once on each side, turn it over and bake another 20 minutes. Voilà! Perfectly baked potato.

Cut the baked potato in half, put a slice of cheese on top and sprinkle on black pepper. Broil halves until cheese melts and bubbles.

Serve hot with rock salt on top, if desired.

Serves 1. Multiply at will.

Accompaniment
Endive, lox and foie gras salad; cornichon pickles; riesling-marinated jalapeño garlic cloves

Wine
Fischer bière d'Alsace (amber); Rosé de Marlenheim; edelzwicker

Pommes frites

Patrice Suhner, "*currently planning his next venture . . .*" Vancouver

Not so much a recipe as a method. These are frites Patrice, the vraie *thing, the best anywhere. Even if you've abandoned the humble frite in favor of more fashionable starches, this will bring you right back. For years, when he was the cooking partner at Vancouver's delightful Café de Paris, Patrice would send these out unbidden with virtually everything he served save the soufflé glacé. I rarely saw any going back to the kitchen—certainly not from my table. When he sold the place and went back to France there were still frites there but they weren't quite the same. I don't know why. He doesn't either. He did come back to cook in the kitchen with the best view in the country, probably the world: at Windows on the Bay in the Coast Plaza Hotel, thirty-something stories above the bay in Vancouver's West End. His menu was more Mediterranean, more elegant than bistro fare, but he was known to whip up a batch of kidneys in mustard sauce and a sizzle of his signature fries on request. I'd always request.*

> 2-2¼ lbs / 1-1.25 kg jumbo russet
>   potatoes
> Canola oil for deep frying
> Salt to taste

Accompaniment
Maybe a little more
salt . . .

Wine
Plonque; bière

Peel, slice lengthwise, and cut potatoes into ¼-⅜-inch-wide (5 mm-1 cm) sticks. ("I like the ⅜ myself," says the chef.)

Place cut potatoes in a large bowl of cold water. Change water repeatedly to remove the potato starch, until water remains clear. This can be done ahead.

Before cooking, dry potatoes well with a clean dish towel. To cook the first time, heat oil to 350°F (180°C) in a deep fryer, or the typically French (and politically *dangereuse*) black cast-iron pot with the removable basket, known as a *negresse*.

Fry potatoes in small batches until completely cooked but barely colored, shaking occasionally. Remove and set aside.

Note: In order for both the interior of the potato to cook completely and the exterior to crisp without burning, it is necessary to fry the potatoes twice. They can be fried several hours in advance the first time and the second time, just before serving.

Reheat oil to 350°F (180°C). Fry potatoes without crowding them too much (otherwise they'll steam) until crisp and golden brown. Transfer to a big bowl, sprinkle with salt and serve immediately.

Serves 4.

Lemon and Parmesan Oven-roasted Potatoes

This is one of the recipes that arrived as if by magic or osmosis, meaning no one remembers where it came from or whose handwriting it was in the first place. It's probably a family secret of Julia Child's or someone similar and the lawyers are already on the phone about it.

I think this came about as a discussion with long-time DiscDrive *technician Grant Rowledge, one afternoon, during a long piece of Mozart. I'll leave my little room and go into the bigger part of the studio and we sometimes compare recipes.*

On my last birthday the women and cat in my life cooked me a surprise dinner, wherein this was only one of five—count 'em—five potato dishes. There was leek-and-potato soup, potato skins with gloppy cheese sauce and diced smoked goose breast; tiny red potatoes in an aioli with an attitude; and the following. Dessert was an immense angel food cake with fresh strawberries and parsley.

The cat did not participate in the cooking but did add his mellifluity to the song of celebration that accompanied the wheezing-out of the candles.

4 big potatoes (Yukon Golds)
2 Tbsp. / 25 mL olive oil
2 Tbsp. / 25 mL unsalted butter
Black pepper
2 Tbsp. / 25 mL lemon juice
4 Tbsp. / 50 mL parmesan
     (or half each parmesan and Asiago)
Lots of parsley, chopped
Coarse salt on the side

Scrub potatoes with a vegetable brush. Slice ¼ inch (5 mm) thick or even thinner and drop into a bowl of cold water as you slice. Soak for 30 minutes to 2 hours.

Line a big cookie sheet or two with foil. Put oil and butter on the sheet and heat in a 450°F (230°C) oven until butter melts.

Drain potatoes and pat dry. Place potatoes on the cookie sheet and toss to coat with oil and butter. Spread them out as much as possible. The crunchy ones are the best, so they want lots of direct-heat surface area to cook in.

Sprinkle with pepper and bake 15 minutes. Turn slices and sprinkle with lemon juice and cheese. Bake another 10 to 15 minutes, turning once more, until they are golden brown (longer if you want them crunchier).

Sprinkle with parsley as they're served. Dip in coarse salt before eating if you like.

Makes enough for 2 at my house; maybe 4 normal people.

Accompaniment
Nothing

Wine
Okanagan Springs Pale Ale (it was my wedding ale, after all); or Krug Clos de Mesnil Champagne

Pancetta Mashed Potatoes

Wolfgang von Wieser, *Chartwell, The Four Seasons Hotel, Vancouver*

Over Christmas 1992 I did something I've never done in forty-mumble years of Christmas dinners. Ate out!

Yup, we did that. Sans child, sans cat, sans friends and relations.

More to confess. We didn't feel the slightest bit guilty once we'd got our heads around the concept. We did the Roast Goose that Ends the Year at home on Christmas Eve. The reason the roast goose ends the year, kitchen-wise, is that after it's done, the oven is useless for anything except sanding down and Tremcladding as a porch planter. We forget about it until the cleaning frenzy that heralds the new year and eat a lot of boil-in-the-bag pheasant-salad sandwiches.

And so it came upon a Christmas Day. The child sent overseas for "Christmas 2: The Relatives," the cat sent under the bed with a yule log full of fresh shrimp, the relatives sent cards and letters, while ma in her kerchief and I in my cap sent ourselves to The Four Seasons' Chartwell for dinner.

This was not without some effort. The idea, you see, came to us only two days earlier, between fierce bouts of shouting over who'd used the last of the Scotch tape.

"D'you think we might want to go out for dinner on Christmas Day?" It

sounded almost heretical. But there. It had been said. It was out.

"Gee, I dunno," the idea fascinating, if outré, "Do you?"

"I dunno. I asked first. Your call."

You know how that all goes. But once we grabbed hold of the idea it began to feel pretty good.

So I called Chartwell. Yes, there are three dinner sittings, fixed menu, fixed price: 3 o'clock, 5:30 and 8:30. But it looks like they're all full. Could they maybe borrow a little bar table from the Garden Lounge, say, and set it up against a wall, and sure we'd happily take the 3 o'clock and we promise not to show up with three extra last-minute guests.

A table was found, laid, positioned by the Chartwell fire even, under that painting of Sir Winston's place—all warm and cosy candles aflicker, ice bucket nearby, basket of lavash and breads on the table.

The menu read beautifully. Join me if you want, and sound all the conso-nants with smackage of lip: home-smoked salmon, swordfish and tuna with horseradish cream; Québec tour-tière with juniper-braised red cabbage; tiger prawns steamed with ginger and crisp vermicelli. There's a kind of Emily Dickinson quality to the cadence if you do it nice and stately.

Peppered duck consommé with apple ravioli. Then beef filet with mar-row glaze, spiced butternut purée; or pan-fried Dover sole with potato-arti-choke rissole; or turkey roasted with

Accompaniment
Christmas turkey;
roast sirloin; roast
chicken

Wine
Burgundy of modest
means

marjoram, brussels sprout leaves and cranberries. Winter greens salad and then Valrhona dark-chocolate mousse with plum compote and vanilla cream; Christmas cookies and truffles with the coffee.

I do not mean to demean a lifetime of moms—mine, yours, anybody's—but this was probably the perfect turkey. And why did those mashed potatoes not merit a mention on the menu? They deserve commemorative postage stamps, and you wouldn't even need those fancy holograms, either.

And the fire warmed the room and the Sterling Three Palms Chardonnay warmed to the room, and we warmed to the Sterling and all the other tastes that paraded across the palate like something out of a culinary Ice Capades.

And there were little girls in velvet dresses with lace who sipped stuff through straws and grandmothers in regal mauve, and all manner of adults grinning around the table and babies announcing their pleasure in a corner alcove and new gift ties and kimonos and more. It was as festive as anything I can recall.

This recipe was brought out by hand from The Four Seasons kitchens.

1 lb. / 500 g potato
1/4 lb. / 100 g pancetta (Italian bacon)
3 Tbsp. / 45 mL whipping cream
1 Tbsp. / 15 mL butter
Sour cream
Salt and pepper to taste

Boil potatoes in salted water until soft. Drain and mash or rice. Keep warm.

Slice pancetta thinly, place on a baking sheet and cook in oven until crisp. Alternatively, pancetta can be diced and sautéed in a frying pan until crisp and drained afterwards. Cool pancetta slightly and chop fine. Warm whipping cream and beat into potatoes. Add butter, sour cream to taste and pancetta. Season to taste.

DRINKS

I would!

Four Monks In Trouble: An Anti-Vampiric or: Blueberry-Garlic Spritzer, Mark II

Who says there's never anything good on television? The original version of this recipe was "an almost-accidental creation in a television interview with Dan Bagnani and Mitzi Ayala on a station in Sacramento," according to my source of the drink, California wine country chronicler Mildred Howie. Bagnani was one of the pioneers in the modern California wine industry; his family established a winery in San Francisco following the repeal of Prohibition, opening the original Four Monks Wine Vinegar plant across the street.

Later he purchased Geyser Peak winery and after its sale in 1971 concentrated on the vinegar side of things until the company was sold to Nakano Vinegar of Japan. The first recipe used raspberry vinegar and sparkling water. Caterer Marcia McKeegan came up with the blueberry version for a vinegar tasting in Cucamonga. Finally Mildred Howie sent me the instructions and here it is.

I can't believe I actually made this at my restaurant-book launch and served it to five of the city's best chefs. None of them rushed right up and asked for the recipe with a view towards serving it at their restaurants. That's all right; they were probably just too shy, so here is their second chance.

½ cup / 125 mL simple syrup
   (¼ cup / 50 mL sugar dissolved in the same amount of boiling water)
1 medium garlic clove
3 Tbsp. / 45 mL Four Monks blueberry vinegar
6 cups / 1.5 L seltzer or soda water
6 fresh or frozen blueberries for garnish

Before syrup gets too cool, crush pulp and juice of garlic clove into it. Let syrup stand for half an hour, stirring occasionally. Strain through very fine sieve to remove solids. Fill six 10-ounce (300 mL) glasses half up with crushed ice. Add 4 tsp. (20 mL) of garlic-syrup mixture, 1 ½ tsp. (7 mL) blueberry vinegar, 1 cup (250 mL) seltzer/soda to each glass. Garnish with a blueberry. Do not set on fire!

Enough to frighten 6.

Accompaniment
Whatever you dare

Wine
I would!

The Simpsons: Bart and Lisa

Brent Wolrich, *The Salmon House, West Vancouver*

Say ciao Shirley, and let her sink. That was my sentiment early in 1994 when I put out a call to get a kids' drink or two happening that wasn't (A) based on ginger ale; and (B) named after a sixty-years-ago curlyhead. Cheery but weary, that one.

It happened one night at the Salmon House on the Hill. The wine had been ordered. Now, what do you have as a non-alcoholic drink, asked The Child at the Table. Well, said the server, all happyfaced and stepping into tonight's minefield, we've got a Shirley Temple, or . . .

Yuck! went the Child with conviction in her voice, the eyebrows millimetering up, the right corner of the lip Presleycurling, the whole body language clanging Disdain! Disdain!

Too right, I thought. Time to give this holdover from the '30s a decent non-denominational burial. These are kids who cut their baby teeth on the bionic cutesters Mary-Kate and Ashley. They chuckle at the secret-society high-fives of the Fresh Prince. They've got the skinny on everybody in Melrose Place. Plus they know more about birds and bees at ten than you and I did going into our second marriage. At 10 we didn't even know

enough to ask where that ditzy expression came from.

Of course it wouldn't have mattered much if we had asked. We'd just get shunted to the other member of the parenting team, who was trying to doze in front of the Dozen Detroit Dancing Dentists on Sullivan.

There's something innately yuckworthy to the old connotation. To say nothing of the visual association. You know full well no self-respecting child past the age of six months would voluntarily request one as a pre-dinner drink. What would The Brain, say? Pinky? Narf, indeed.

So the call went out, in a "Carte Blanche" column and it was the selfsame Salmon House's man-about-the-bar Brent Wolrich who responded first and best. The drink recipes were tested and focus-grouped to an au courant Grade 5 class who had responded with these survey results: 40 per cent said citrus as the principal flavor; 35 per cent, chocolate. Eighty per cent said no to things floating in it but yes to bubbles. Thirty-six per cent liked orange, 24 per cent, tropical fruit, 72 per cent wanted ice, 84 per cent, a straw, and so on.

Meet Brent's Bart and Lisa. Have one yourself, you'll be surprised. Rumor has it he's retooling the Lime Rickey, fast-forwarding the Gin Fizz . . .

The Lisa Simpson

1 very tall glass, half full of ice
1 oz. / 30 mL orange juice
1 oz. / 30 mL pineapple juice
½ oz. / 15 mL grapefruit juice
2 oz. / 30 mL cranberry juice
7-Up
Garnish

Mix all the juices with the ice. Top up glass with 7-up. Garnish with a slice or wedge of orange and a sword "to ward off boys."

To paraphrase the inimitable Lisa, "No cherries, no grenadine; it's soooooo bad for you."

The Bart Simpson

1 very tall glass, half full of ice
1 oz. / 30 mL orange juice
½ oz. / 15 mL pineapple juice
1 oz. / 30 mL grapefruit juice
Cola
Grenadine syrup
Cocktail cherries
Orange wedge

Mix all the juices with the ice. Top up the glass with cola. Splash in "tons of grenadine," add 2 cherries and a wedge of orange stuck on a sword.

"Why? 'Cuz I like it that way, man!"

Each recipe is for 1. Adjust for volume by octupling or punch-sizing, as needed.

Accompaniment
Appetizers, snacks, pizza, calamari, whatever they're eating

Wine
Buy yourself a nice bottle to drink while you watch them fight it out across the table with those swords

Eshcol Wine Warmers (in Both Official Colors)

Trefethen Vineyards, Napa, California

Elsewhere in this collection we use Trefethen's excellent Eschol proprietary blends in cooking, dessert and such. Here they are again in the cold-weather version of the cooler. We call 'em "warmers," as is only fitting, and we make them with fruit, spices, warm wine and other tasty ingredients to take the chill off after skiing or just generally flailing about in the snow.

⅂ **Accompaniment**
Any sort of cold-weather nibblies

Wine
It's always safe to stick with the main ingredient: in this case, either color of Eshcol

Red Version

6 cups / 1.5 L Trefethen Eshcol red wine
1½ cups / 275 mL fresh raspberries (or frozen unsweetened)
6 slices orange
3 slices lemon
9 cloves
1¼ cups / 300 mL sugar
1 Tbsp. / 15 mL black peppercorns, whole
1 star anise, whole
Orange peel, kumquat slices, more raspberries, mint, for garnish

Place everything except the garnish in a saucepan and bring to a boil. Lower heat and simmer gently 20 minutes. Strain through sieve or cheesecloth, pushing down on the ingredients. Pour into mugs and garnish with fruit. Serve hot.

White Version

1 cup / 250 mL sugar
½ cup / 125 mL water
4 cups / 1 L Trefethen Eshcol white wine
2 cups / 500 mL apple juice
4 slices lemon
2 vanilla beans, slit
2 2" / 2.5 cm pieces of cinnamon stick
5 cloves
Powdered cinnamon, freshly grated nutmeg, more cinnamon sticks for garnish

Put sugar and water in a saucepan and cook over low heat until sugar dissolves and mixture is clear (about 5 minutes), swirling the pan occasionally. Turn up heat and boil until sugar caramelizes and turns a deep brown. Stand well back from stove while pouring in wine and apple juice (mixture will splatter). Add lemon slices, vanilla beans, cinnamon sticks and cloves. Bring to a boil again, lower heat and simmer gently for 20 minutes. Strain through sieve or cheesecloth.

Pour into mugs, garnish and serve hot.

Each recipe serves 4.

Grace's Delight

Located by Hugh Quetton, and
found in his book of drinks for all days,
I'll Drink to That

*Pretend, just for now, that it's
September 7th, which also happens to
be my brother Peter's birthday—so I'll
just take this opportunity to wish him
a happy one, in case I forget the card
again.*

*Any September 7th will do but the
year happened to be 1838 and there
was William Darling and all his vol-
unteer boatmen of County Durham,
rowing their way through monstrous
seas to find a foundering steamer run
aground. Talk about a disappointing
gig: nobody was on board when they
finally arrived. The crew had already
been rescued by the keeper of the
Longstone light and his cronies. To
make matters worse, it was William's
older sister, Grace, who got the
Humane Society's lifesaving medal
'cause she got there first, being one of
those cronies.*

*So this drink would certainly cheer
the crew—or anybody else out on a
night like that.*

3 ½ oz. / 105 mL Scotch whisky
4 ½ oz. / 140 mL sweet (red) Vermouth
1 ½ oz. / 45 mL raspberry brandy
Juice of 1 orange
3 juniper berries, gently bruised
Pinch cinnamon
Pinch nutmeg

Pour whisky, vermouth and raspberry
brandy over shaved ice in a jug. Add
orange juice, juniper berries, cinnamon and nutmeg. Stir it all up with a
silver spoon. Strain into a cocktail
shaker. Refrigerate at least 1 hour.
Shake before serving.

Share with at least one other
person.

113

Accompaniment
Nibblies

Wine
Not right now,
thanks

114

Apotheosis of the Summer Slush (Mature)

Finding myself with a freezer full of a particularly pleasant Gelato Fresco one summer, and harboring a nagging feeling that here was one of the best ice cream creations the world has yet seen, I sat down to apotheosize the summer slush, the Slurpee, the float, the soda. Not for those about to operate any heavy equipment or those under the age of majority.

½ oz. / 15 mL Finlandia vodka

½ oz. / 15 mL Cointreau

½ oz. / 15 mL Ava Tahiti eau de vie de pamplemousse (not always easy to find except at the Papeete duty-free in Tahiti, so just double up on the Cointreau!)

3 scoops Gelato Fresco Sicilian Blood-orange Sorbet

Whirl everything in the blender for 10 seconds. Drink with a long-handled spoon.

"Two on the deck in the late afternoon, and I'll say good night."

For 1.

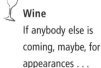

Accompaniment
Something elegant, decadent and not too hard to peel

Wine
If anybody else is coming, maybe, for appearances . . .

Cranakvavit

*One of the best ways I know of enjoy-
ing the healthgiving properties of the
modest cranberry is this simple project,
wherein all the work has already been
done for you by the distillery.*

*Try to keep the cat from poking a
paw through the plastic wrap to whack
at the berries.*

**1 bag fresh cranberries, washed and
   picked over**
1 bottle akvavit

Put the berries in a big glass bowl.
Pour akvavit over. Save the bottle. Let
the bowl sit on the kitchen counter,
with a plate or some plastic wrap to
cover, for a couple of weeks or until
you get just too curious. Take out the
berries with a slotted spoon (keep
them on hand for a tasty condiment
with a kick) and pour akvavit back in
the bottle.

Into the freezer it goes (don't lay it
down flat, it may leak) for the better
part of an afternoon.

By the time dinner guests arrive
you can greet them with an icy shot
of pink, cranberry-zapped schnapps.

Accompaniment
Pickled herrings of
all kinds; iced shrimp

Wine
More of the same

Bloody Nonsense: A Garden Kick

Accompaniment
Crudités, spicy dip; chips, guacamole, pita bread, anything remotely Mediterranean

Wine
After the sun goes down

I'm told that the Bloody Mary is still the number one vodka drink in the U.S.A. Here in Canada we sip on Bloody Caesars, a decidedly Canuck creation as you will know if you've ever tried to order one on Ozark Airways. But if you further refine the ingredients, adding the caraway zip of akvavit, say, and the fuller-flavored tang of vegetable juice, why, you come up with this, as I did one spring afternoon. I think Bloody Nonsense is as good a name as any. If you can't find the green Trappey's, a bolt of plain old Tabasco will do.

1 lemon slice
½ tsp. / 2 mL chives, chopped
3-5 drops Trappey's Hot Jalapeño Sauce (green)
2 drops Angostura bitters
2 drops Worcestershire sauce
1 oz. / 30 mL akvavit, from the freezer
Garden Cocktail vegetable juice
Ice cubes

Drop lemon slice into the bottom of a tall glass and sprinkle in chives. Drop Trappey's, Angostura and Worcestershire on lemon slice. Pour on frozen akvavit. Fill up glass with Garden Cocktail. Plop in a few ice cubes to maintain coldness.

Fall about the garden later, if the spirit moves you.

Serves 1.

DESSERTS

And why should it be pronounced the same as the word for "abandon or give up"? Especially since I never can?

118

Boysenberry Pyramids & Savory Cheesecake

Janet Trefethen, *Trefethen Vineyards, Napa, California*

These are two separate dishes but for some reason they are always linked in my mind and in my kitchen. If you do them both, there's not much else required for lunch except the wine and the bread. The famous blends of Trefethen, called Eshcol, and used elsewhere in this collection as wine "warmers," are wonderful and virtually unknown outside of California. The winery is a super spot to visit as part of your Napa travels. The guest house is in the most gorgeous vineyard setting. But that's another story . . .

Accompaniment
Each other, with a lemon-light oil-poppyseed vinaigretted simple salad in the middle

Wine
Try Eshcol white (or a Napa chardonnay) with the cheesecake; something late harvest and sweet with the pyramids. Maybe that same Sauternes

Savory Cheesecake

¾ cup / 175 mL breadcrumbs, toasted
¾ cup / 175 mL walnuts, toasted and chopped
3 Tbsp. / 45 mL unsalted butter, melted
¾ lb. / 350 g Asiago or tomme cheese, grated
1¼ lb. / 625 g cream cheese
4 eggs
1 medium garlic clove, crushed
1 tsp. / 5 mL fresh or ¼ tsp. / 1 mL dried tarragon, minced
Pinch salt and pepper

Combine breadcrumbs, walnuts and melted butter in the food processor, mixing well. Press the mixture into the sides and bottom of an 8-inch (20 cm) springform pan and set aside.

With an electric mixer, beat the grated cheese together with the cream cheese. Add 4 eggs, one at a time, beating well after each addition. Add garlic, tarragon, salt and pepper, and mix.

Pour the mixture into the crust and bake at 350°F (180°C) for 45 minutes or until cheesecake is firm in the center. Let stand 30 minutes before serving.

Boysenberry Pyramids

Cream

½ cup / 125 mL crème fraîche
2 ½ Tbsp. / 35 mL mascarpone cheese
1 Tbsp. / 15 mL sugar

Whip the crème fraîche into soft peaks. Beat in the cheese and sugar. Refrigerate until ready to use.

Syrup

7 cups / 1.75 L large fresh
 boysenberries
⅓ cup / 75 mL sugar
2 Tbsp. / 25 mL Sauternes

Sprinkle 3 cups (750 mL) of the berries with sugar and Sauternes. Cook over medium heat about 20 minutes, until thickened. Allow mixture to come to a boil and then reduce heat, stirring gently. Set aside.

Pyramids

3 sheets phyllo dough
2 Tbsp. / 25 mL melted butter
1 Tbsp. / 15 mL ground almonds
1 Tbsp. / 15 mL icing sugar

Brush a sheet of phyllo with melted butter and sprinkle with sugar and almonds. Cover with a sheet of phyllo and repeat. Top with the third sheet and sprinkle with powdered sugar. Cut rounds of stacked phyllo 4½ inches (11 cm). Bake on a cookie sheet at 350°F (180°C) until barely golden, 5 minutes or so. Cool.

Spread each round with mascarpone cream. Dip remaining berries individually in syrup and mound on top of cream to form a pyramid. Drizzle syrup all around.

Serves 6.

120

Sunburnt Lemon Pie

Pierre Delacôte, *Seasons in the Park, Vancouver*

This one's tart and intense like a lemon meringue pie without the meringue, the top sugar-crystallized until the whole thing's almost a wedge of lemony crème brûlée. Pierre serves it on big white platters with multicolored sugars and syrups and flower petals.

The freshly zested lemon taste is wonderful after a big meat dish—a roast leg of lamb, perhaps. It bites right through and leaves the palate all fresh and cheery.

Seasons is where Clinton and Yeltsin dined during the Vancouver summit, and home of the now-internationally known fresh blueberry tart with maple ice cream. Clinton, maybe—but I'm sure Yeltsin's never eaten such a good dessert since.

Crust
   1 cup / 250 mL all-purpose flour
   ¼ cup / 50 mL granulated sugar
   ⅓ cup / 75 mL butter
   1 egg
   1 Tbsp. / 15 mL orange juice
   1 tsp. / 5 mL orange rind, grated

Lemon Filling
   ¾ cup / 175 mL granulated sugar
   6 eggs
   ¾ cup / 175 mL whipping cream
   ½ cup / 125 mL lemon juice
   2 tsp. / 10 mL vanilla
   1 tsp. / 5 mL lemon peel, grated

Accompaniment

Maybe a little extra dollop of cream? (On the Flying Scotsman, from London to Edinburgh, I was offered extra cream for my cheesecake!)

Wine

A glass of Okanagan late-harvest optima or Vancouver Island ortega; Quady Essensia would be especially good

In food processor, combine flour and sugar. Using on/off pulser, cut in butter until mixture resembles coarse meal.

In a small bowl, combine egg, orange juice and rind. Add all at once to flour mixture. Mix in just until dough forms ball. Refrigerate 20 minutes.

Press dough into greased 11-inch (28 cm) flan pan and place on baking sheet. Cover pie with parchment paper and fill with pie weights. Bake shell in 350°F (180°C) oven for about 20 minutes or until center is set. Remove weights and parchment paper.

Meanwhile, reserve 1 tsp. sugar. In a bowl whisk together eggs and remaining sugar. Whisk in whipping cream, lemon juice, vanilla and lemon peel, until smooth. Pour into shell and bake 30 minutes. Let cool.

Sprinkle reserved sugar over pie. Cover edge with foil. Broil for about 3 minutes or until sugar is dark brown.

Serves 8.

Kentucky Bourbon Bread Pudding (Pouding à la Jacques Daniel)

Bernard Plé, *Hyatt Regency Hotel, Vancouver*

How does that old Chinese adage go again? The one about being careful what you wish for 'cause you just might get it? I've long had trouble keeping my mouth shut. When half a million people are witness to one's ramblings it can get dicey. It's what led me into performing Walton's Façade *with a chamber ensemble, when Masterpiece Music founder Linda Lee Thomas heard me mutter something about always having wanted to try it. Bang! Next step, on stage in front of a live audience and it wasn't Kansas any more.*

So too with Bernard Plé's remarkable Kentucky Bourbon Bread Pudding, which I had at the Hyatt one night. It was sublime. So sublime that the next day on DiscDrive, I raved about how I'd cheerfully dive into a whole swimming pool full of the stuff.

Time passed.

But the Hyatt's then-PR person, Nancy Spooner, had heard and filed my wish for future reference. Later, on the occasion of my birthday, as I sauntered into the office after doing my regular daily broadcast, there were people and candles and shouts of Surprise!! and Happy Birthday!! and damn it all, there was a swimming pool full of bread pudding!

It was a kid's plastic wading-pool, to be precise, but it held enough bread pudding to feed all those assembled and anybody else I would encounter for weeks. Slabs of it went into a holding pattern in various freezers for later, gleeful consumption.

The bread pudding is, I'm happy to say, still on the menu at the Hyatt Hotel's Fish & Co. restaurant. Bernard made the recipe available to listeners who clamored for it and here it is again for wider circulation.

When we did DiscDrive Live with the Vancouver Symphony I talked a lot about how much I liked Lamborghinis . . .

3 large eggs
1¼ cups / 375 mL sugar
1½ tsp. / 7 mL nutmeg
1¼ tsp. / 6 mL cinnamon
¼ cup / 50 mL butter, melted
2 cups / 500 mL milk
½ cup / 125 mL raisins
½ cup / 125 mL pecans, chopped and dry roasted
1 oz. / 30 mL bourbon
5 large slices French baguette

Whip eggs and sugar together. Add nutmeg, cinnamon and melted butter. Beat in milk slowly. Stir in raisins and pecans. Add bourbon

Line bottom of 2-quart (2 L) casserole with baguette slices. Pour mixture over the slices (pan should be half full). Bake at 400°F (200°C) for 20 minutes.

Serves 1!

Accompaniment
Whipped cream

Wine
A glass of Lynchburg's best or a tot of brandy

122

Double Chocolate Mashed Potato Brioche with Almond-Caramel Sauce

Rodney Butters, *Wickaninnish Restaurant, Tofino*

🍴
Accompaniment
A hearty dinner

Wine 🍷
Quady Elysium;
Greek mavrodaphne;
Keo Commandaria,
from Cyprus; a sweet
sherry or a light ruby
port

Rodney Butters is the new breed of chefs: born here, trained here, works here. He wants to be one of the very best in B.C. He hasn't got far to go. Like others of his culinary generation he's creating what we are coming to call "Canadian cuisine" and he's more than proud of the fact.

"I think it's high time to be focusing on Canadian cooking . . . " Which to him means fresh, light, flavorful, good and good for you—food from right around the neighborhood, up and down the coast. His marvellous dinners can be unrepentant carnivores' delights or dazzlingly daring vegetarian creations or just about anything in between.

If there's a criticism it must be that the meals are often too filling to allow even the most determined among us room for dessert. And so, back when he was in town at the Monterey Lounge & Grill, it took me three tries before I got around to this one. The chef calls it his signature dessert, having had it on every menu and planning to keep it on every one to come. "My grandmother used to make something similar," he says.

So here's your chance.

Brioche
5 oz. / 140 g bittersweet chocolate
1 Tbsp. / 15 mL instant coffee
3 Tbsp. / 45 mL amaretto
½ cup / 125 mL butter

4 large eggs, separated
½ cup / 125 mL granulated sugar
1 cup / 250 mL mashed potatoes
½ cup / 125 mL almonds, ground
Pinch salt
½ cup / 125 mL chocolate chips

Melt chocolate, instant coffee, amaretto and butter over a double boiler. Beat egg yolks with sugar until thick and creamy. Add chocolate mixture until blended. Add mashed potatoes and ground almonds until thoroughly combined.

In a separate bowl, beat egg whites until stiff. Fold egg whites and chocolate chips into batter. Pour into brioche molds and bake at 350°F (180°C) for approximately 30 minutes. Let cool for 15 minutes and remove from molds.

Sauce
⅔ cup / 150 mL sugar
¼ cup / 50 mL water
½ cup / 125 mL whipping cream
4 Tbsp. / 60 mL slivered almonds, toasted

Dissolve sugar in water in a pot. Caramelize sugar to golden brown. Heat cream and add all at once to caramel. Add toasted almonds and cool.

Serve warm brioche with sauce and dark and white chocolate shards.

Serves 8.

Peaches with 2 Ortegas and Saint-André

Ortega is one of the new German wine hybrids that have found particular purchase on Vancouver Island, where four wineries vie for the favors of the locals, and also in the Fraser Valley east of Vancouver.

Loretta Zanatta first alerted me to the gustatory pleasures of her ortega alongside sliced fresh peaches. When I found the rich, barely botrytized late harvest version from my friends the Violets at Domaine de Chaberton, I knew I was onto something.

And so I urge you to get lots. After all, the sweeter version makes the marinade for the fresh fruit, and the peaches must be bursting ripe. What you don't finish at one sitting you will want to be sipping at around 2:30 A.M., when you've just awakened from your first good REM snooze and are wondering what might soothe you back to sleep.

Do not pour any in the cat's dish. He'll lap it up and then lick his paws and push them over his ears and get his head all sticky and in the morning when you come out for coffee you'll find him glued to the bottom of the fridge door.

4 large super-ripe peaches, sliced
2 oz. / 60 mL Domaine de Chaberton Botrytis-affected Ortega
Wedge of ripe Saint-André or brie cheese

Peel and slice peaches. Place in a single layer in a flat dish. Pour ortega over. Let stand at cool room temperature or in the fridge for 3 to 4 hours. Turn peaches a couple of times.

Bring cheese to room temperature.

Serve peaches in a small glass bowl with the marinating ortega, and the cheese on a matching small plate.

Serves 2.

123

Accompaniment
Portuguese-style corn bread; Tuscan crusty bread

Wine
Vigneti Zanatta Cowichan Valley Ortega

Strawberries Romanoff with Russian Cream (Old Foolproof)

Some years ago, to launch my book on favorite Vancouver restaurants, I let two otherwise wonderful women named Terri Wershler and Elizabeth Wilson persuade me to cook a multi-course meal, in public, for five Vancouver restaurateurs, all of whom were represented in the book. Some of the other dishes are also in this book— you'll have to try and find them on your own. Were the chefs impressed? "The aperitif left a lot to be desired." "The prawns were palatable but just barely." "The lamb was passable." "But the dessert was to die for." That last comment came from Amyn Sunderji, who is one of the fifteen greatest people in the universe. Of course you know how to make this. Everyone knows how to make this. It was a favorite of the cats, who thought for a long time that Strawberries Romanoff were little ripe berries covered with a spoonful of Petrossian's best. Their disappointment at discovering the composition of the real thing was immense, but in typical feline fashion, brief.

Lots of red, juicy, fully ripe strawberries (don't make this with those steroidy ones that have the white patches near the stem)
½ cup / 125 mL berry sugar

Equal tots or any combination, to make up a good ½ cup (125 mL) or more: Triple Sec, vodka, Doorly's Barbados Amber Rum, eau de vie de fraise (or framboise), Whidbey Island Vineyard and Winery Loganberry Liqueur, Grand Marnier
1 cup / 250 mL whipping cream
½ / 125 mL cup sugar
1 Tbsp. / 15 mL unflavored gelatin
½ tsp. / 2 mL pure vanilla extract
1 cup / 250 mL sour cream

Slice strawberries or leave whole, your call. Sprinkle with sugar. Pour booze on. Marinate in a cool place as long as you can stand it, stirring every so often.

Heat whipping cream, sugar and gelatin over very low heat until gelatin dissolves. Cool, add vanilla and sour cream and mix thoroughly. Cover and chill for 6 hours or longer (put some clingy wrap over it if it's going in the fridge next to the salmon overnight).

To serve, spoon some berries and marinade over the bowl of Russian Cream and let people scoop out their own. Another way is to put cream in individual ramekins and serve one for each person.

Serves 6 who've eaten a fair bit and now want something light to finish.

Accompaniment
Some of those crispy little rolled-up French dessert wafers you get with your ice cream at that wonderful place on the Île St. Louis, whose name I can't remember right now

Wine
Something very late in the harvest from the Okanagan. Upending the strawberry bowl into your glass may not be elegant, but it is rewarding.

Lemon Mousse

Anne Milne, *chef/consultant, Vancouver*

For years I carried this recipe around with me, in Anne's original handwriting. I'm pleased it has finally found a somewhat more permanent place; the yellow newsprint has come to fade quite a bit.

It is so good, so tangy and fresh and zappy and zippy and all those other z-words that fussbudget foodwriters like to use—and they aren't even playing Scrabble—and so easy. Anne says it can be made with limes instead, and she has "whittled this version . . ." because her original, for 24, yields voluminous amounts of mousse.

5 eggs
1 cup / 250 mL sugar
⅛ lb. / 60 mL unsalted butter
(½ stick), melted, then cooled
1 cup / 250 mL freshly squeezed lemon juice
2 cups / 500 mL heavy cream
1 Tbsp. / 15 mL lemon zest, blanched

Combine eggs and sugar and whisk until pale in color. Beat in cooled butter, slowly. Add lemon juice. Cook mixture in stainless steel bowl over a pot of boiling water, whisking constantly until it thickens, about 10 minutes.

Remove from heat and cool in fridge for 1 hour. Stir a few times as it cools. Whip the cream stiff and add the zest to it. Fold into the cooled lemon custard. Pour or pipe into dessert glasses.

Adapted from the original for 24, to make 6 to 8 desserts.

125

Accompaniment
Biscotti

Wine
Calona Pinot Blanc,
Burrowing Owl
Vineyard

Chocolate Cake Sandwich for Kids' Lunches

My fondest school memories center on the opening of the lunch bag to find a real surprise. In those days such surprises didn't need to be all that elaborate, just something different between two slabs of bread was fine: a touch of unexpected garnish; a home-baked goodie for recess. Different but not outré was the way to go. After all, there was that moment of truth when the others asked, so, what have you got today? Nobody wanted to say steamed tripe with crenshaw melon relish on a coulis of smoked cilantro.

Lunch surprises of sufficient appeal that all the containers come back empty, that's the ticket. Lunchmakers must be ever mindful of the fact that kids tend to be the most conservative of creatures, that the thought of doing, saying, wearing or even eating anything original is absolutely infra dig. Secretly they're angling for tasty treats that don't always focus on spongy white bread and cheese byproducts.

But given the fact school lunches still mostly do revolve around two slices of bread with stuff in between, there are various ways to address this old standard with imagination. A slab of focaccia sliced through the middle, spread with cottage cheese and piled with avocado, grated parmesan, sunflower

sprouts and toasted Caesar-salad croutons is one. How about a slice of whole wheat and a slice of white, with cubes of cheddar, Monterey jack, edam and Gruyère stacked in between?

Get an epi loaf, separate the little thinglets, slice 'em up and fill each one with something different: peanut butter and kiwi; shaved ham and marbled cheese; cheddar and mayo; tuna mashed with celery but NO onion; flaked chicken and hot dog relish; wieners sliced lengthwise with circus mustard. There's a sandwich six-pack. Or this . . .

2 slices raisin bread
Danish Orchards Cherry Conserve
Nutella hazelnut-chocolate spread
1 slice chocolate cake with icing
Crushed M&Ms (or sundae-topping
  sprinkles)
1 very ripe sweet peach or plum, sliced
Marshmallow topping

Spread one slice of bread with the cherry conserve. Spread the other slice with Nutella. Scrape icing off top of chocolate cake and spread it over the whole cake slice instead. Put the cake on the Nutella half of the bread. Throw on the M&Ms or sprinkles, or both. Add fruit slices in overlapping rings. Put on a dollop of marshmallow topping. Slap both bread slices together fast so nothing can fall out. Wrap tightly with plastic wrap to hold everything in (unwrapping and eating are not *your* problems).

Serves 1.

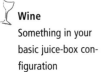

Accompaniment
Barbecued potato chips; Zoodles out of the Thermos; carrot sticks

Wine
Something in your basic juice-box configuration

Minted Chocolate Pastry Shards

Bernard Casavant, *Wildflower Restaurant, Chateau Whistler Hotel*

I was invited to be a guest host at a Nutrition Month cook-off once.

I didn't much want to go, pointing out to the charming and persistent person who'd got to me in the first place that I didn't got out to eat for the sake of health. I go out to eat forbidden food and, generally, pig out.

She wanted to convince me I could eat the cake as well as having it and so I did do the deed and came away believing it could be done. Of course, it helped that there were a dozen top-flight chefs in the competition cooking their nutritious hearts out.

Chateau Whistler's Bernard Casavant, who can be found at most competitions and celebrations, was one of those chefs. His dish was a sensational dessert: grilled organic pears on rhubarb risotto (pink grapefruit juice was the cooking liquid!), a little mascarpone cheese folded in with some strawberry preserves, and these minted chocolate pastry shards.

It's the sort of sweet I don't ever recall my mother exhorting me to eat up or I wouldn't be allowed to have any broccoli! Things have changed.

⅓ cup / 75 mL margarine (you *could* use butter!)
¼ cup / 50 mL pure maple syrup
1 Tbsp. / 15 mL cocoa powder
2 tsp. / 10 mL peppermint, chopped
3 sheets phyllo pastry

Melt margarine and add maple syrup, cocoa and mint. Lay first sheet of phyllo on surface and brush with syrup mixture. Repeat with second and third sheets of phyllo. Bake at 350°F (180°C) for 8 to 10 minutes until crispy. Break into shards to accompany dessert dishes.

Serves 6.

Accompaniment
Poached grilled pear, pink rhubarb risotto and strawberry orange preserve. (All are Bernie's recipes, and a jaunt to Whistler and a visit to his Wildflower Restaurant will yield those too. Call ahead.)

Wine
Quail's Gate Okanagan Chardonnay

128

Kahlua-fried Bananas

Corinne Poole, *Giraffe, White Rock*

As West Coast seaside restaurants go, Corinne Poole's Giraffe, in White Rock, is among the more unprepossessing and among the best. The chef holds forth in a kitchen the size of a Buick glove compartment with a patch of fresh herbs, lots of local produce, a couple of cats and a headful of wonderful ideas about cooking and combining flavors.

Can I interest you in a little plate of veal medallions with sour cherry sauce and Peruvian mashed potato salad? Cardamom pound cake with Grand Marnier-and-passion fruit sauce and spiced mascarpone? It's a wonder there aren't a couple of complimentary Thigh Masters out front.

If Corinne's little restaurant were somewhere in the French countryside there'd be Maseratis and Mercedeses from all over the E.U. parked out front. Don't forget to take lots of change to feed the City of White Rock's greedy little all-night parking meters, or you'll get a ticket.

Corinne has one of the most creative sweet teeth in the business. This dish is simplicity itself until you get to the add-on options, at which point you can go crazy, as she often does.

Accompaniment
Well, Corinne serves it with warm chocolate cake at her seaside restaurant . . .

Wine
Any of that Kahlua left?

1 nugget butter
1 banana (cut in half lengthwise, then in half again, i.e., 4 pieces)
Sugar
Generous splodge Kahlua

Garnish
Toasted pecans, chocolate sauce, mint flowers, chunks of pineapple and papaya

Put nugget of butter into a non-stick pan and heat over medium. Dust banana pieces in "plain, old-fashioned" sugar. Place pieces sugar-side down onto pan. Sizzle over medium heat until caramelized to your favorite crispiness. Flip over and heat bananas on other side.

Arrange banana pieces on an attractive plate. Deglaze pan with Kahlua. Flambé with gas if you have it, otherwise light Kahlua with a match. When flames go out—we have sauce!

Sprinkle with pecans and mint flowers, pour on chocolate sauce and arrange fruit chunks on the side of the plate.

Serves 1.

STUFF

*Things that
chanced along and had
to go somewhere.*

Adventures in Tourtière: The Lyons vs the Pikes, etc.

As will become clear presently, this is a joint venture, whose principals are Mayne Island realtor Jill Pike and radio host (Classical 96/103 FM, in Toronto—he made me put that in) Michael Lyons.

Traditions have to start somewhere. This one is a tradition-in-the-making, only a few Christmases old at the moment, but becoming a December event to look forward to. It centers on the humble-but-oh-my pie from Québec.

Why tourtière? Taste, first and foremost and always. Plus the fun of making a dinner in the kitchen that everyone can get involved in—even the cat—without it becoming a major sauce 'n' curdle kind of enterprise.

It takes the better part of the afternoon and by the time the sky is getting dark and the lights start to come on around the house, it's ready. The place smells sensational. The cat stomps around muttering vague threats about leaving home, but for good this time, if he doesn't get some of that ground meat in his bowl now—I mean NOW!—even if they do muck it up with that cinnamon and stuff.

The Child of the House is repeatedly peeled from the ceiling. She would consider going to bed this minute, if only she could sleep, to speed up the passing of the night. Never mind the solstice, this is the longest night of the year.

Like most good traditions, this one developed, evolved, from several sources. The menu is usually the same: soup, tourtière with two veggies (one red, one green), dessert, cheese, shortbread, pecans, chocolates and on into the night.

The choice of drink is also diverse. Yop! because that's the COH's preference (Canadian Springs is best for the cat); E. D. Smith's Garden Cocktail (although I don't see old Smith's name on the label anymore) dead-cold, with a squeeze of lemon and a dash of iced akvavit, for the grown-ups. Labatt's 50 in the quart bottles if we could find some, but that Fischer beer from Alsace is fine. Wine? If you want, some moderate red, whatever's in the house; this isn't that kind of dinner.

The pie, the crust, the foundation of the tourtière has three influences. First, a basic recipe (as well as the insistence on the E. D. Smith) from my old colleague Michael Lyons's mother. The crust is the work of Mayne Island's Jill Pike. The final mix of meat and seasonings is tuned after a read-through of the Montreal Gazette's *Julian Armstrong's* work on Quebecois cooking.

Accompaniment
Cream of fennel and oyster soup; marinated brussels sprouts; crunch-cooked red cabbage with apple and vinegar and caraway; chocolate-cream bûche de Noël

Wine
See story

Cat
Large Manx

Crust

 4 cups / 1 L all-purpose flour
 1 lb. / 500 g butter (margarine, if you
    must), chilled
 1 cup / 250 mL sour cream

Cut butter into flour until it's all
coarsely mealy. Stir in sour cream
with a fork, until just blended. Dough
will be soft so chill for a couple of
hours, then roll out the top crust
between layers of waxed paper.
Refrigerate that while rolling out the
bottom. Mold into pie plates and
think about the filling. This is enough
for two double-crust pies.

Filling (for a double-crust 9" / 22.5 cm pie)

 1 lb. / 500 g lean ground pork
 1 lb. / 500 g ground veal
 2 onions, chopped
 ½ cup / 125 mL consommé, more or
    less
 Salt and pepper as needed
 Generous sprinklings of cayenne,
    ground cloves, mace, cinnamon

Brown the meat in a big pan. Add
onions and sauté until translucent.
Stir in everything else, mixing well,
and let cool. Spoon filling into pie
shell and cover with top crust.

 Bake at 425°F (220°C) for 15 minutes, then turn oven down to 350°C
(180°C) and bake another 25 to 35
minutes, until the crust is golden
brown and you can't bear the aroma
any longer. Cool if you have the
patience, slice and eat.

 Serves 2 to 4.

Rās al-Hānout

In Morocco this is the all-purpose spice, flavoring tajines (stews) with or without meats. My favorite is just steamed cauliflower drizzled with a little melted butter and seasoned with rās al-hānout. Like harissa, it's one of those mixes you'll wonder how you ever got along without, once you start using it.

Accompaniment
Stews, meats,
vegetables,
couscous, rice

Wine
Some unapologetically
raunchy Moroccan
red; fresh-leaf mint
tea with lots of sugar

1 tsp. / 5 mL cumin
1 tsp. / 5 mL ginger
1 tsp. / 5 mL coriander seeds
1½ tsp. / 7 mL black peppercorns
¼ tsp. / 1 mL cayenne
4 cloves
4 allspice berries
1½ tsp. / 7 mL cinnamon

Blend all ingredients in a spice mill or disused coffee grinder 'til powdered fine. Keep in tightly closed jar, away from the light, for 6 months or so—then you need to make a fresh batch.

Double, quadruple or raise to any other power to make as much as you need.

Corncob Jelly

Jayne Wagner,
The Village Cheese Mill, Salford, Ontario

This came home from southern Ontario one summer when my wife went to visit her family. As part of the same trip came an antique rocking chair which, I'm sure, taxed Air Sarnia's cargo hold to the max. Most amazing was the fact Air Canada misplaced the luggage between there and here, and the rocking chair arrived in the company of various valises around 1:30 in the morning, in a van bound for Whistler loaded with ski equipment that had also been sidetracked. The rocker sat on the front porch until morning, wrapped suggestively in newspaper and decorated with "fragile" stickers, but there was no doubt about the contents.

But back to the jelly. With a pale but tangy Ontario cheddar, this proved to be a smashing combination. No one seemed to know what corncob jelly was all about, though the name ought to have given a clue. No recipes from central Canada, no amount of Mennonite kitchen research managed to turn up any reference. What else was there to do but ask The Answer Lady. (The Chicken Music intro, and a voice says, "And now, The Answer Lady, Marg Meikle . . . ")

Ms Meikle answers questions from listeners to Vicki Gabereau's afternoon CBC *program once a week. Somehow, we managed to get through to her and*

she called Jayne Wagner and got the straight goods. Actually, it was my sister-in-law Janet who tromped down the road to Jayne's place near Wallaceburg, and got it handwritten out on green paper.

The cheddar is a must.

12 cobs fresh corn
6 cups / 1.5 L water
Lemon juice if needed
1 box Certo pectin
3 cups / 750 mL sugar

Take corn off cob and reserve for other eating. Put water into a pot with the cobs. Bring to a boil and simmer 20 minutes. Remove cobs and put through a jelly bag to strain out any corny bits left.

Bring 3 cups (750 mL) corn juice and pectin to a boil. If there's not enough for 3 cups, just add more water or a little lemon juice. Add 3 cups sugar and bring to a boil again. Boil for 1½ minutes.

Take a little jelly out of the pot and cool a little on a tablespoon. Pour off the spoon 'til drops join together and pour slower. When it's reached this stage, bottle it.

Accompaniment
Tillsonburg aged white cheddar and any kind of crackers

Wine
Tawny port; Washington merlot

Oven-baked Garlic

Once upon a time there was a splendidly silly—and very good—Vancouver restaurant called The Frog and Peach. Yes, after the skit. No, neither pêche à la frog, nor frog à la pêche was on the menu; the Cointreau bill would have been horrendous! While the F&P provided dozens of dandy dishes, it was the baked garlic with melted brie on top that became one of my serious favorites. You could tell it was a favorite of others too, because a block down the street was an art-movie house. Many's the night that many of us sat there watching Ingmar Bergman flicks while clouds of garlic wafted all about us.

There's not a lot to cooking a whole head of garlic but it's nice to be able to do it with fresh garlic. The dry kind with the papery covering is fine, but the flavor of fresh is something else again. Given that garlic season in early summer is relatively short around here, there's a narrow window of opportunity during the year. This'll fill it.

Save the oil. It's wonderful for sautéeing vegetables, meat, anything.

Accompaniment
Nothing but bread is needed.

Wine
Whatever you think might cut the garlic—probably red, probably Mediterranean. Probably cheap!

Any number of whole heads of fresh garlic
Olive oil
Fresh thyme
Black peppercorns
Brie (rind cut off) later

Cut a slice across the top of the garlic heads. Peel off the outer skin. Put the heads in a small baking dish so they are touching, root side down. Pour some oil over and sprinkle herbs and peppercorns on top. Cover the dish with foil and bake for 30 to 40 minutes at 300°F (150°C), basting now and then. Check for doneness by poking one of the cloves. It should be mushy.

Continue baking, foil-covered, for another 15 to 30 minutes, depending on the size and freshness of the garlic. Take garlic heads out of the oil. Put a generous blob of brie on top of each head and return to the oven or microwave to melt the brie.

Serve at least one per guest or eat everything yourself.

Fresh Basil Vinaigrette

Ernst Dörfler,
Five Sails, Pan Pacific Hotel, Vancouver

Yes, it's a very simple little dressing. Sure, you could probably have figured it out yourself. But Ernst Dorfler already did it and here it is. It sat beside a fresh green salad at a July lunch commemorating U.S. Indepen-dence Day. There were foods to cele-brate regional cooking of all parts of the U.S. and they were all very nice. But the taste I took away with me was this dressing and I forewent my cus-tomary inclination to double up on the real Boston Cream Pie and had three helpings of salad instead. Then I went to lie down and soon felt much better! I phoned the executive chef the next day and his simplicity-itself instruc-tions arrived. This is for a family-sized salad.

> 6 Tbsp. / 90 mL extra virgin olive oil
> 2 Tbsp. / 25 mL lemon juice
> ½ medium shallot, chopped
> ¼ medium garlic clove, chopped
> 4-6 fresh basil leaves, chopped
> Salt and freshly crushed white pepper
> to taste

Put all the ingredients in a bowl and mix well. Chop the basil leaves just seconds before you assemble the dressing so they don't discolor. Dresses a few generous salads.

Accompaniment
Good fresh greens: frisé (curly endive), mâche (lamb's let-tuce), arugula, sorrel, escarole, etc.; slow-butter-fried-in-a-cast-iron-pan croutons

Wine
Sparkling water with lots of fresh lime slices

Cheese Sables

Dr. Irene Hain, *Kitchener-Waterloo,*
Ontario

I went to Kitchener-Waterloo for the first time ever in the early part of 1995, to do the first Wine Auction and Tasting for conductor Howard Dyck's Kitchener-Waterloo Philharmonic Choir. I took along a box of wine, ate well, went to the farmers' market and bought Mennonite sausage, conducted the auction, and we raised all sorts of money for the choir's trip to Europe. It was a good way to beat the mid-February blahs.

This is where I met Irene Hain—country doctor, cat lover, wine appreciator and Ferrari driver. At a dinner at her house the evening after the auction, she surprised and delighted me by bringing forth a 1919 Château Haut-Brion, which I was asked to decant. My right arm hurt for a week! The wine was a wonderful bit of history and a grand treat and we polished it off smartly with a roast beef dinner, following it with some of Serge Hochar's fascinating Château Musar from Lebanon.

But at the beginning of the evening, as I was trying to engage the cats in meaningful conversation, there were these cheese crispies on the table along with other nibblies. I must have devoured several dozen. I asked Irene Hain to send me the recipe.

"As usual," said her faxed note the next day, "I adapted two or three

recipes to make one. Perhaps I made that last batch with a bit too high a proportion of butter, but this is what it by rights should have been."

½ cup / 125 mL all-purpose flour
½ tsp. / 2 mL paprika
¼ tsp. / 1 mL dry mustard
Pinch cayenne
4 Tbsp. / 60 mL butter, softened
4 oz. / 125 g cheddar or Gruyère or
 Imperial packed cheese, grated
1 tsp. / 5 mL Worcestershire sauce

Mix the dry ingredients. Work in butter. Add cheese and Worchestershire. Chill for 30 minutes. Cut into ¼-inch (5 mm) slices. Cook on a foil-covered cookie sheet for 8 to 10 minutes at 350°F (180°C). Lift foil off tray immediately after removing from the oven and let cool before lifting finished product. Store in airtight tin.

Share with a cat is my suggestion.

Accompaniment
Olives, smoked oysters or mussels, smooth paté

Wine
Simple white or light red

Hot Garlic Dip (Bagna Cauda)

Robert Le Crom, *Hotel Vancouver*

Italy's famous "hot bath" for cold vegetables depends on the kick of garlic and butter and anchovies to make it work. Serve it at the table on a hot plate or even a fondue pot to keep the bagna nice and cauda, but not boiling. This, because you'll be dipping cold raw vegetables in it, like a fondue.

½ cup / 125 mL butter
¾ cup / 175 mL oil
4-6 garlic cloves
anchovy fillets, puréed
Pinch salt

Heat butter and oil over medium heat. Add garlic, lower heat and cook 10 minutes. When garlic is very tender add anchovies and stir everything together. Add salt if it isn't salty enough for you.

For a plate of vegetables for 4.

Accompaniment
Celery, Belgian endive, turnips, savoy cabbage leaves; red and green pepper strips blanched in a little vinegar. Carrots are not recommended. Broccoli? If you must . . .

Wine
Hofstätter Gewürztraminer from the north of Italy; Valdizze Pinot Frizzante Naturale; a couple of cold cans of Moretti

Miss V's Tuna Ephemera

Vicki Gabereau, *Vancouver*

The last word—a bit of a poignant tale, really—belongs to my delightful just-down-the-hall colleague who is heard, at times directly opposite me, on The Other Network of the CBC. Vicki Gabereau full-nelsoned me into giving her a recipe for her cookbook, so I made her give me one for mine.

As you know from listening to her (and reading her cookbook), she doesn't cook, so she claimed not to have a recipe. I knew differently, having watched her fling a skirmish of haggises into the oven on New Year's Day and everybody else in the room an astonishing number of sheets windward.

Hence this. Well, she's right—it isn't a recipe at all. It's a plea from the soul for assistance; it's a reminiscence of childhood à la recherche du temps perdu; a Madeleinian moment of introspection on a theme of canned fish. Who's to belittle its import? Religions have been founded on scantier premises in the past.

Ms G. has had more food prepared in her studio than I in mine. She's also got a couch in hers and a lot of cute decorator touches, while I've got zip, even though my ratings are the highest on the network I'm on, but hey! who's bitter? I think, though, I've had better service, what with full-course meals made by chefs from the Hyatt and cat-encrusted cakes from The Four Seasons, and martinis and torta rustica from The Raintree and wading pools full of bread pudding.

But I digress. Miss Vicki is that rarest of creatures: a Vancouverite. It's my secret suspicion that's the sole reason she didn't win the election as mayor of Toronto; they wouldn't have been able to stand it.

Her story starts as a little tyke, growing up in Kerrisdale, going to Quilchena school. "My parents both worked and so my grandmother lived with us and looked after me. It meant," recalls Miss V fondly and who wouldn't, "that I could do damn near anything I wanted."

And what she wanted was tuna sandwiches. Not peanut butter and jelly, not bologna and Kraft slices, not ham 'n' lettuce, not walnuts and brie on peppered foccacia (none of those things had been invented yet anyway), but tuna, for lunch, at school, every day.

She claims that "nothing but tuna" is what she had every day from about Grade 2 until just before she left. "Tuna all the time, unless there was something eventful, like a Thanksgiving turkey in the house."

And she was happy in her ichthyological singularity. But there is a lament. The reason for this plaintive cry from the soul is that she has never been able to make a tuna sandwich like her grandmother.

"*She probably used 'way too much mayonnaise—or most likely, Miracle Whip*," recalls La Gabereau. "*And of course, it has to have Worcestershire sauce in it. My grandmother would open a tin of tuna, drain off the oil (I'm sure there wasn't such a thing as tuna packed in spring water), rinse the tuna, and then scrunch it all up in a bowl, put in a great glop of the mayo or MW, Worcestershire, and black pepper.*"

Celery? I interrupt, and she throws up her hands in horror. "*My God no! And white bread, of course.*" *Of course. But now grandmother is making sandwiches somewhere in the Great Cafeteria in the Sky. Vicki keeps trying here below, in the vale of tears 'n' tuna.* "*I get so upset they're not the same,*" *she deprecates.*

And so, basically, this is a your-idea-goes-here recipe. Help fulfill Vicki Gabereau's life before the millenium ends. What's the missing ingredient, or procedure? I don't know either. Let me recap what we know so far.

2 slices pre-sliced white bread, crusts cut off (optional)
1 can oil-packed tuna, drained and rinsed
1 glop mayonnaise or Miracle Whip
1 dash Worcestershire sauce
Some black pepper

AND?

Open the tin, drain off the oil, rinse the tuna, scrunch it all up in a bowl, add the glop of mayo or MW, add Worcestershire and black pepper and enrobe in two slices of bread

AND?

Thank you very much.

139

Accompaniment
Another one

Wine:
(Your choice goes here)